GREEN PLACES *in* SMALL SPACES

GREEN
PLACES
in
SMALL
SPACES

A Practical Guide
to Designing and Planting
a Small-Space Garden

Kerwin Fischer

The Taunton Press

Front cover photographer: ©Ken Druse
Back cover photographer: Derek Fell

First printing: March 1997
Printed in the United States of America

The Taunton Press, 63 South Main Street,
PO Box 5506, Newtown, CT 06470-5506

Created for The Taunton Press by Storey Communications, Inc.,
Schoolhouse Road, Pownal, Vermont 05261

Library of Congress Cataloging-in-Publication Data

Fischer, Kerwin
        Green places in small spaces : a practical guide to designing
    and planting a small-space garden / Kerwin Fischer.
            p.   cm.
        Includes index.
        ISBN 1-56158-184-4 (hardcover)
        1. Flower gardening. 2 Container gardening.   I. Title.
        SB405.F57 1997   96-50491
        635.9—dc21   CIP

For Andrea

Contents

Acknowledgments

I WOULD LIKE TO THANK all those who helped and supported me in this project, in particular the Parish of Calvary/St. George's, the Reverend Dr. Thomas Pike, and my vicar, the Reverend Stephen Garmey, who had the trust and faith to choose me as his plantsman, for which I shall be ever grateful.

I also want to thank Mrs. Simon Strauss for her endowment of the Calvary Church garden as a memorial to her parents, Winifred and Mark McCloskey, which makes it possible for the work to progress; Joseph Butler, Calvary Church sexton, who makes everything I do easier; and my able garden assistants, Valerie Osborne and Jennifer Barrows.

Others whose input was essential include Brian Coats and Beverly Moore for their support and photographic help; Tom and Ellen Mann for their encouragement and discerning eye; my great friend Carolina Edwards, who gave me the benefit of her publishing experience; and Cherilyn DeVries of The Taunton Press, my very kind and patient taskmaster, for her gentle guidance and assurance.

I would also like to mention in remembrance Ernestine Day Fischer, my mother, whose love of garden and greenhouse inspired the same in a certain small boy, and her devoted gardener, Fred Langevin, whose patience with small boys is legendary.

Finally, I thank Andrea King, my wife and partner, whose loving encouragement made this book a reality.

Introduction

LOTS OF CITY DWELLERS dream of the day they'll have a place in the country to grow flowers, the day all those winter evening dreams over plant catalogs will come true. But you don't need five acres in the country to have a garden. If your condominium or apartment has a balcony, a deck, or a little enclosed space, you can have a garden. If there's a strip of grass by the curb, you can grow flowers in it.

You can create a garden in a few square feet of soil almost anywhere, and if you pay any attention at all to it, it will thrive. I'm not kidding. Once in a small town in Vermont, I saw a tiny strip of ground between the sidewalk and the street sown with a wildflower mix. It was stunning. I have seen a garden growing in the median strip of Broadway on New York's Upper West Side. It flourishes in spite of the street life. People garden in tiny plots around sidewalk trees, by the front stoops of apartment buildings, on patios of suburban town houses, in window boxes, and on every available rooftop. As I look out my sixth-floor office window, I can see two fair-size copses on rooftops within a hundred yards. I know a man who has a lovely and peaceful garden six floors above East Eighteenth Street in Manhattan. He has more beautiful things growing on that tiny roof than are in most one-acre yards. And, I might add, it is more peaceful than most one-acre yards.

My own garden is located at the corner of Twenty-first Street and Park Avenue South beside an old brownstone church. Actually, it belongs to Calvary Church and is entrusted to my care. It is large for a city garden, approximately 20 by 60 ft., something over 1,200 sq. ft. Still, it's not hard to run out of growing room, and every year I wrestle with myself over what to keep, what not to keep, and where I can squeeze in a few more bulbs. I will never be able to try everything I really want to grow.

It is just as rewarding as any suburban flower garden might be, perhaps even more so, because it's very concentrated, as smallish gardens must be. And consequently, it attracts some attention. I may spend an average of five or six hours a week maintaining it in the summer. During that time, 10 or 12 people stop and tell me how much it means to them to have a little bit of the country in the city. A lot of others stop and look. Many say they take the long route home so that they can watch the garden's progress every day through the seasons. Sometimes it's hard to get much work done because of all the visitors.

Some of the comments are very wise, and I'm amazed at how many with gardeners' souls live among these concrete canyons. Others wax poetic. Recently, following a particularly hard and gloomy winter in the Northeast, a well-attired elderly gentleman with a British accent stopped to admire the spring plantings and recited this verse from memory:

I wandered lonely as a cloud
That floats on high o'er vales and hills,
When all at once I saw a crowd —
A host of golden daffodils
Beside the lake, beneath the trees,
Fluttering and dancing in the breeze.
 — William Wordsworth, 1807

It means a lot to the neighborhood, I think, providing a sort of rallying point, common ground that everyone cares about. I guess that's because plants make people feel good. After all, city life is still a very new development in the history of humankind. Maybe we need some contact with the natural world to keep us in the right frame of mind.

The garden is on one of the busiest corners in the city. All day and all night cars, buses, and trucks blow the by-products of hydrocarbon combustion through the iron fence and onto the plants and soil. People throw things into it and pull things out of it through the fence ("harvesting," we call that euphemistically). Yet the garden not only survives, it flourishes. It begins in February or March with the first snowdrop and ends with the Japanese toad lily and some diehard astilbes and sedum in November or December. In between, it progresses through its bulb period to its blue period through its yellow period to its pink and purple period with a kind of subdued flamboyance. It is somewhat Victorian in its outlook, on the verge of being cluttered . . . but not quite; a little bosky . . . but not frayed. It fits the old church just fine.

This book is designed to do several things. First, it's a guide to help you get started gardening, anywhere. Size shouldn't be a deterrent. Neither should poor soil; you can live with it, or you can fix it.

Second, it will help you decide what kind of a garden is right for you and what you can grow, given the conditions. No sun? No problem! You can have a lovely garden for three full seasons and even part of a fourth.

Third, it will help you to plan for a succession of bloom in your garden, from thaw to frost. This is the most difficult part about designing and maintaining a flower garden. When I see pictures of a beautiful bed of tulips, I always wonder what it looked like two weeks later. No flower blooms for the entire eight or nine months that the garden is active in the more temperate zones of the United States, so it's necessary to have several stages of bloom follow one another in the same spot. This book will tell you how to do that.

This is not a technical book. We will not be talking about the morphology of plants or about the difference between a sepal and a petal. Any good book on botany will provide you with that information. This book will not list every plant that you could possibly grow. It is simply a practical, hands-on map to help you get started growing things in your small plot.

WHAT'S IN A NAME?

Even though this is not a technical work, you should be aware of the official names for plants. These are formulated by the International Union of Biological Science and are constructed in an obscure language called Botanical Latin. Botanical Latin bears little resemblance to classical Latin. It is derived mainly from Renaissance Latin with a smattering of Greek thrown in (I suspect just to make it more indecipherable to laypersons like you and me), and it is truly understood only by botanists. However, familiarity with the proper scientific name will help ensure that you get what you really want.

Each plant has a *genus* name, which is always capitalized, and a *species* name, which is usually not capitalized. The name *Iris sibirica* says first that it's an iris and second that it originated in northeast Asia. Similarly, *Cypripedium reginae* means "the queen's slipper," usually translated as "showy lady's-slipper." Subsequent references to the same genus customarily use only the first letter and a period, followed by the species name (*C. reginae*).

Sometimes you will see a third name. This is the *variety* name, which is usually descriptive and never capitalized. It also indicates that the plant will reproduce "true" from seed—that is, be the same as the parent. For example, *Campsis radicans flava* tells us that this *Campsis* produces aerial roots (*radicans*) and that it's yellow (*flava*).

When you see an x in the name, it means that this is a hybrid, a breeding between two species. Seeds of hybrids might not come true—that is, look exactly the same as the parents. In *Aster* x *frikartii*, we can tell that this is a hybrid aster developed by the Swiss Frikart Nursery.

Most hybrids are created by crossing two species. Rarely, a cross is made between two genera, as in x *Pardancanda norissii*, 'Park's Candy Lily'. You will notice that the x comes first in this case because the hybrid is a cross between *Pardanthopsis* and *Belamcanda*, two distinct genera.

There also may be a fourth name (you don't often see all these names together) called the cultivar, from *culti*vate and *vari*ety. It is always in Roman letters and in single quotation marks. It represents some mutation in form or color that has happened while the plant has been in cultivation, hence *Daphne* x *Burkwoodii* 'Carol Mackie' is a happy genetic accident that occurred in gardener Carol Mackie's New Jersey backyard, though many cultivars may be selections propagated vegetatively.

Many scientific names of plants have to do with the discoverer's name (see *Puschkinia*); some are commemorative, such as *Franklinia alatamaha*, the Franklin tree; many are only vaguely descriptive (*Allium pulchellum* simply means "pretty little allium"); and others may

BASIC BOTANICAL NOMENCLATURE			
Cypripedium GENUS	*reginae* SPECIES		
Campsis GENUS	*radicans* SPECIES	*flava* VARIETY	
Aster GENUS	x (HYBRID)	*frikartii* SPECIES	
x (HYBRID)	*Pardancanda* GENUS	*norissii* SPECIES	
Daphne GENUS	x (HYBRID)	*burkwoodii* SPECIES	'Carol Mackie' CULTIVAR

concentrate on some obscure feature (*Phlox subulata* tells us that this phlox has awl-shaped leaves; it does not tell us that it makes a great ground cover for hills and banks or that it is low growing and forms a beautiful floral blanket).

Names of cultivars can be anything. While some are descriptive and others commemorative, many are absolute nonsense. Names such as 'Itsy Bitsy' or 'Twinkle Toes' are appended by growers who hope to spur sales because the names are cute.

It is not necessary to know what scientific names mean, but they are constantly thrown around by people in the plant world (most of whom don't know what they mean either). And since they *are* common parlance (and are consistent, which common names and cultivars often are not), you will have a much easier time finding a specific plant if you know its Latin moniker.

Don't worry about how to pronounce these names. Since no one speaks classical Latin conversationally anymore, no one really knows.

Now you are ready to join the legion of gardeners who are driven to prevail no matter what the obstacles. Concrete: no problem! Traffic: who cares? Let the gardening commence!

The Calvary Church garden in early April.

CHAPTER 1
Evaluate Your Space

THE SITE YOU CHOOSE for your garden will largely determine what you can grow there. You should consider the following factors:

- The amount of sunlight the site gets, especially in spring and summer
- Rainfall (or how you're going to get water to it)
- Exposure to stressors (Is it sheltered from wind, vandals, animals, etc.?)
- Time

Plants flourish in the most unlikely places, from desert to Arctic tundra. Some lichens even grow *inside* rocks in the McMurdo Dry Valleys in Antarctica. So even if you have little or no choice about where to locate your garden, take heart. Something, probably *many things,* will grow there.

SUNLIGHT

The amount and intensity of available light is a factor for all gardeners, but most rooftop and patio gardeners have a little more flexibility than others, as their gardens have some combination of sun and shade. Even in a small area, you can grow any number of flowering plants in 10-in. pots and just place them where they will get the light they need. For a large area, a collection of such plants may not be enough. You might want to add some small trees to the mix.

This will provide some contrasting heights to your arrangements of pots and make the space much more pleasing to the eye.

WHAT IS YOUR "LIGHT BUDGET"?
- Check the light each hour of the day over a period of months.
- Note the "blackout" times.
- Make a chart indicating areas of light and shade.

Most plants need some light to feed themselves through the process of photosynthesis, which produces carbohydrates. Some need a lot of light, some just a little. Before you decide what you're going to grow, you need to spend some time studying the light and the possibilities it offers. This will save you a great deal of time and money later replacing plants that have failed in your particular conditions.

Make a Light Budget

Look at your potential garden site at every hour of the day over a period of time, March through June, for instance, and remember that light will vary depending on the time of year. Judgments you might make about the light in March probably won't be valid for June or July, when the sun is much higher in the sky. Check the light at 9:00 A.M. one day, 10:00 A.M. the next day,

SOME PLANTS FOR SUN

ANNUALS	PERENNIALS
Calendula	Black-eyed Susan
California poppy	Clematis
Cleome	Daisy
Coneflower	Daylily
Gazania	Iris
Lisianthus	Liatris
Marigold	Peony
Nicotiana	Phlox
Petunia	Poppy
Salvia	Rose

SOME PLANTS FOR SHADE

ANNUALS	PERENNIALS
Begonia	Astilbe
Caladium	Columbine
Daphne	Fern
Impatiens	Globeflower
Pansy	Hosta
Vinca	Lenten rose
	Lily
	Lobelia
	Toad lily

and so on. Make a chart of which areas of the garden get mostly bright light and which are in shade. This is important because you need to know the total hours of sunlight the site gets in the course of a day.

For example, my corner looks very sunny at 10:00 A.M. and 3:00 P.M., but in the middle of the day (prime sun time for plants such as irises and peonies), it's in shade, the whole plot in the shadow of a large building across the street. Consequently, I have difficulty with irises and peonies in all but the sunniest part of the garden. I wouldn't even consider trying to grow salvias, poppies, or other plants of the open meadow there. But some very prolific bloomers love partial shade—plants such as some lilies, daylilies, campanulas, and astilbes. These are some of the mainstays of my partially shady urban patch.

Evaluate the Direction of the Light

The direction of the light is important, too. North light is great for artists' studios because there's no direct glare. But in your garden, north light means you will get little or no direct sunlight. This doesn't mean you can't have a garden; it just means you'll have to stick to plants that don't need direct sunlight. Hostas and ferns are obvious choices, but there are

The Sun at Noon in January

The Sun at Noon in July

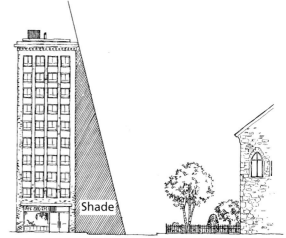

Shade

Garden

Shade

Garden

many others: Trollius, or globeflower, the domesticated version of a native American wildflower, produces lovely golden blossoms in deep, damp shade; the great blue lobelia, which has 3-ft. stems of deep blue flowers, thrives in shade; and the well-known forget-me-not does just fine in shady situations.

An eastern exposure obviously means that you'll get the morning light. This generally produces a cooler environment than afternoon exposure and is good for hostas, columbines, and even impatiens. Many lilies, particularly the species (nonhybridized, or wild) lilies whose native habitat is the edge of woods, will do well here, as will daylilies.

A western exposure means bright (and often burning) afternoon sun. Depending on other conditions, meadow lovers such as daisies and centaureas will do well here. Poppies also will like this situation, as will salvia (meadow sage), black-eyed Susans, purple coneflowers, and cornflowers. Bright-colored annuals such as zinnias, marigolds, petunias, and sunflowers like the afternoon sun, too, as long as there's enough water for them.

A southern exposure gives the most flexibility because in the Northern Hemisphere you get some morning light and some afternoon light. It's also the brightest exposure overall. Lots of plants will do well here, except those for which full sun is a must, such as delphiniums. If you happen to have the western sun as well, go ahead and try these plants.

Unless you live in Manhattan, where virtually everything is oriented directly to the compass points, you will probably have some combination of exposure directions. That's why it's so important to see what's going on in your garden at each hour of the day and to plan accordingly.

Watch the light not only in the total garden but in the various parts, too. Even in 4 sq. ft., the light can differ dramatically. The shade of a tree, for example, can make shade-loving impatiens the right choice for one half of the garden and a sun-loving salvia perfect for the other.

Evaluate the Shade

While you're evaluating the shade, think about what kind of shade it is. A big oak, maple, or beech tree will give a shade too deep even for impatiens. Only a deep woodland wildflower

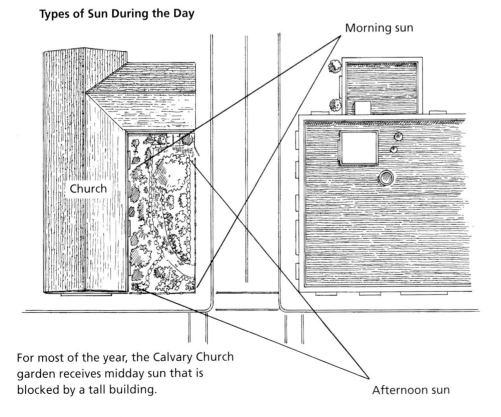

Types of Sun During the Day

Morning sun

Church

For most of the year, the Calvary Church garden receives midday sun that is blocked by a tall building.

Afternoon sun

A tiny stream supports a variety of woodland plants. (Photo by Alan Detrick.)

This sunny border shows dramatic use of height and color. (Photo by Karen Bussolini.)

A hot and sunny spot calls for natives of the open meadow. (Photo by Karen Bussolini.)

such as mayapple would think of growing there, and even it needs some light. (Sometime, drive down the Blue Ridge Parkway in Virginia in spring. You will see many shaded dells filled with mayapples.)

A birch, crab apple, or pine will likely give dappled shade, and lots of plants will do well there, including ferns, impatiens, hostas, and many of the spring bulbs, such as dog's-tooth violet (also known as trout lily), English and Spanish bluebells, and small fritillaria. Lots of native American wildflowers, such as jack-in-the-pulpit and Solomon's-seal, also will flourish in these circumstances. They make great conversation pieces and sometimes furnish some great surprises: In the fall, if you look where jack-in-the-pulpit was blooming in the spring, you're likely to see an engaging spike of very red berries that will last right up to frost. These plants are available nursery grown from many reputable dealers and mail-order houses. Please don't go out to the woods to collect them, as their numbers in the wild are shrinking.

One good way to decide what's going to thrive where is to think about how a plant grows naturally. Take daylilies, for instance. Most of the daylilies I have seen grow wild in the partial shade of trees lining the roadside or in full sun along fencerows and ditches. Therefore, daylilies should do well in the partial shade areas of my garden. They do. Similarly, violets don't grow in open fields but thrive in shady areas and along the banks of streams. Daisies, cosmos, and poppies flourish in sunny, open meadows, so if you have little shade, they're probably a good choice.

WATER

Besides sunlight, water is of paramount importance to your garden: Too little or too much means sure disaster.

Rainfall

Check the weather section in your local newspaper to find out the normal rainfall in your area and choose your plants accordingly. Even so, sites will handle rainfall differently. If the soil is hard and clayey, a lot of water will just run off. You can amend the soil at most sites with an additive such as vermiculite or compost to prevent this (see Chapter 3). If the site is near the overhang of a roof, you may have a flood every time it rains. Short of installing or modifying gutters, there's little you can do about this. Choose another site. A small tree such as a birch may deflect the force of a hard rain, giving the plants below a more gentle bath. A big, dense shade tree, however, may cut off lighter rainfall altogether, leaving the ground below dry.

Additional Water

Most garden sites will need additional water at some time during the year. You can carry water to a small site or stretch a hose to it. An accessible outside faucet is something to look for when scouting out your site. Gentle watering in the early morning is best. In most of North America, watering in the evening tends to promote mildew and other fungi, as the water remains on the leaves longer in the coolness of the evening. (The exception is the Southwest, where it is more effective to water in the evening because water evaporates so quickly in the desert heat that there is no time for the plants to utilize it effectively.)

Probably the best solution is a soaker hose connected to a timer. Soaker hoses are made of a porous material that oozes water at a slow rate so that the soil absorbs it well. You can set an automatic timer to turn on the water from two to five o'clock in the morning. Soaker hoses provide gentle watering, don't promote mildew or other fungus growth on the leaves, and keep the soil cool, especially if you use mulch (see Chapter 4). They're also a good way to avoid watering passersby along with the plants, a necessary consideration near a well-traveled sidewalk. But if you have a small plot that's convenient to water, don't invest in soaker hoses immediately. Use the regular hose and see how it goes for a couple of weeks.

Many patio and terrace gardeners like to use a drip irrigation system for their potted plants. A drip system usually consists of a larger hose from the main water supply and a number of small feeder tubes that lead to each pot. The smaller tubes terminate in a bulbous ending that delivers water drop by drop. If you can't find a drip system at your garden store, look in the better garden supply catalogs (see p. 126).

If there is no convenient water supply, you might try the good old rain barrel approach. If you can find an old barrel and clean it out very well, you can use it. If not, Gardener's Supply Company (see p. 129) has a 42-gallon plastic model with a spigot. You can connect two of these and fit the spigot with a hose, for a gravity-fed watering system. The rainwater is free.

Potted plants surround a convenient water source. (Photo by Karen Bussolini.)

Daffodils, hyacinths, and pansies make a great window box show. (Photo by Thomas Mitchell, New England Stock Photo.)

Annual flowers dress up an entrance with little growing space. (Photo by Derek Fell.)

EXPOSURE

Exposure to stressors such as wind, dogs, and inconsiderate people can make city gardening a real challenge.

Wind

If you live in a big city, you probably won't have to worry too much about wind exposure because the buildings act as windbreaks, even on most rooftops. (There's *always* a taller building next door.) But in the suburbs or the country, wind can be very damaging. The obvious reason is breakage, but wind is also very drying, particu-

larly in cold weather. Even hardy evergreens can suffer damage if they're not watered deeply to prevent drying. Locate a garden spot that is sheltered from the prevailing winter winds. In Iowa, for example, where the prevailing winds are out of the west, choose the east side of a structure for planting (Oklahoma isn't the only place where the "wind comes sweepin' down the plain"). Or plant a hedge to create a windbreak for flowers. In New England, choose the south, southeast, or southwest side of a structure, depending on the prevailing winds.

One way to help protect tender evergreens such as rhododendrons is to spray them with an antidesiccant like Wiltpruf. Antidesiccants form a film over the leaves that helps prevent water loss. If the plant is in a particularly exposed site, you can make a simple windbreak by putting stakes in the ground around it and attaching burlap to the stakes to enclose the plant from all sides. Burlap diminishes the force of the wind, but allows the plant to breathe.

Dogs

In the city, dogs are naturally attracted to things that smell like the great outdoors—in other words, plants. Given a choice between the curb and a plant, a dog will choose a plant every time. Some people who are otherwise considerate and intelligent seem to lose all sensibility when it comes to handling their pets in the city. Once a woman walking her dog complained to the Vicar of Calvary Church that his sidewalk plantings looked terrible. When he pointed out that her dog might be part of the problem (the dog was relieving himself on the plantings at the time), she departed in high dudgeon. It's a hazard of gardening in the city, so think of a strategy to defeat it, such as a taller fence or dog repellent. (It *might* work.) Or choose another spot.

People

My garden is on a very busy corner, with thousands of people walking past every day. Passersby throw trash through the iron fence. Homeless people sleep in the garden. I have found bottles, bags of trash, syringes, moving cartons, bags and boxes of clothes, large plastic buckets, cigarette lighters, a basketball, a handful of gold chains, a set of U.S. Navy collar insignia, a Marine Corps tie bar, some fake pearls, an arrow with a nasty-looking metal point, and seven brass police whistles (nice ones . . . made in England) in my garden. Once the ground was covered with white paper carrying the letterhead of the Environmental Defense Fund! The point is that you need to find a spot that's reasonably secure, or you'll be very frustrated.

Don't Get Discouraged

Even if your spirits are dampened, don't give up; plants are remarkably resilient. Here are a couple of cases in point. Several years ago, when my irises were looking particularly good,

some midnight reveler jumped the 6-ft. iron fence and broke them all down by whipping them with a stick. That was very discouraging, but the next year they were back blooming better than ever. (Even so, I cannot recommend the stick as a method of improving iris bloom.) A couple of years ago, the adjacent church commissioned some extensive roof repairs. Without warning, a gang of roofers descended on the garden with tons of equipment and trampled it flat. I was crushed along with it, but the following year the garden was *almost* normal.

TIME

When you select your garden site, take into account how much time you have to devote to it. Gardens always take more time than you think they will, and it would be a shame to see yours weedy and overgrown, languishing in the August sun, because you have bitten off more than you can chew. It's also a year-round job, so be conservative in your estimate.

A good guideline is to assume that the garden will require twice as much of your time as you think it will. Consider that you must keep it watered, cultivated, mulched, weeded, and trimmed. If you skimp or shortchange the garden in one of these areas, it will mean trouble. For example, let's say you forget to water for a few days, and you haven't weeded. The plants you want to do well will suffer, and the weeds will take over. This *always* happens, no exceptions. Weeds are simply very hardy, opportunistic, and aggressive plants. In the wild state, they are kept under control by their equally aggressive neighbors. Most weeds, such as the yellow evergreen oxalis, don't grow well in areas that haven't been disturbed by humans. But your garden flowers are sissies compared to these bruisers. So when your flowers weaken and wilt, the more opportunistic plants that thrive in adverse conditions will march right in and conquer, like Caesar in Gaul: *Veni, vidi, crevi* (I came, I saw, I grew).

Increased height helps the garden fit its background.

CHAPTER 2
Personalize Your Garden

PERSONAL GARDENS should have style. A garden's style is its outlook, its attitude, its spirit, and its personality. The Calvary Church garden has a rather Victorian outlook. Style is the reflection of a lot of thought about space, color, texture, plants and plant combinations, and the feelings you have when you think about what your garden should be like and how you'd like to feel when you're in it or viewing it.

GOOD TASTE IN GARDENS

Unfortunately, many gardens are begun with great intentions but planted thoughtlessly, with garish plants placed at random in straight-line beds, one sadly unrelated plant next to another like some ragtag pirate crew: first a neon pink celosia, then a silver dusty miller, then an orange-and-yellow coleus.

Some things planned with the best of intentions just don't work. I recently saw a cluster of about 50 Russell lupines along a country road. They were absolutely glowering, a war party of pygmies arrayed for battle. Then there are cannas: From a 6-ft. circle on an otherwise unblemished green lawn towers a 7- or 8-ft. jungle of foliage topped off by some little red flowers—'King Humbert' cannas rule in this yard! Worse is a gaggle of hideously pink "ornamental" cabbages lining the front walk, waiting to expose

themselves shamelessly to the hapless visitor. Ornamental, indeed! What are these people thinking? Answer: They're not. There is no master plan at work here.

I don't mean to imply that large cannas or lupines should never be used, but they must be in harmony with the whole yard or garden. If you have a lot of tall background plants, cannas should work just fine; in fact, they can be the tall background plants. What they should *not* be is a giant green volcano leaping out of your lawn. Lupines are fine interspersed with other plants in the perennial border, perhaps even three or four together as a bright accent spot—punctuation at the end of a line. But grouped together in a large mass in a small space, they are very imposing. It is my personal belief, however, that there is *no place* on God's green earth that is suitable for ornamental cabbage.

A SENSE OF STYLE

Finding your garden's style is not difficult. You must simply look at your garden site with a fresh eye and look inward with your inner eye.

Find Your Comfort Zone
Think about your own preferences. What makes you feel comfortable? Do you like things formal or less structured? Is your house or apartment

furnished with antiques or something more modern and functional? Do you like things well ordered, or is an element of clutter normal in your life? Are you more comfortable with Botticelli or Monet? Christopher Wren or Mies van der Rohe? John Donne or e. e. cummings?

Do Some Research

Look at other gardens—not the huge, impersonal gardens planted by teams of city workers, but small, personal gardens. This is not hard. Most gardeners are just dying to show you their gar-

A tiny dooryard garden in the heart of the city.

dens. Ask, "What's that?" and you'll have a friend for life. Also look at the gardens of churches and synagogues in your area. These often contain unusual and expensive plants and are beautifully tended because of endowments. One of my favorite examples of a small church garden is that of St. Bartholomew's Church at Fiftieth Street and Park Avenue in New York City. (Remember the wedding scene from the movie *Arthur?* It was filmed there.) The plantings are absolutely complementary to the Byzantine style of the church.

Use a critical eye and take note of the things you like and don't like. This is also a good time to see which plants are doing well in their growing conditions and which are languishing because of lack of light (or too much). This is best done in early summer, for obvious reasons.

Look at picture books of gardens. My wife does this with decorating books and finds them extremely useful for ideas, theoretically "saving us millions." Although the gardens pictured are incredibly well manicured and photographed at the absolute best moment of the year, and you know deep in your heart that nobody's garden really looks like that, they will give you ideas. All gardens are different, and only you can make the right judgments about yours. That's why introspection is needed.

Help Your Garden Fit In

Your garden's style should fit its surroundings as well. If it's next to an older house (or next to an old church, like mine), you might choose an English cottage garden with lots of old favorites: foxglove, Canterbury bells, English iris, lilies, coreopsis, rudbeckia, and the plant that is ubiquitous in British cottage gardens, lady's-mantle.

Some English roses or even a climbing rose, if you have room for a trellis, might be a good choice. These roses have a long blooming season and, unlike the hybrid tea roses, they won't fall victim to every bug or fungus that passes by.

Think about Color

If your background is a neutral stone house or wall, you might consider occasional splashes of bright color in your perennial border to relieve

St. Bartholomew's garden provides a happy oasis for passersby on Park Avenue in New York City.

the sameness of white or pastel flowers. Phlox 'Starfire' is a deep cherry red that really livens up a border. *Kniphofia*, or red-hot poker, is a startling plant with glowing orange spikes, some varieties with red tips. A whole bed of kniphofia looks alien and hostile, but it's great as an accent plant. *Crocosmia* is another good choice, especially the cultivar 'Lucifer', which grows to 3 ft. and has intensely red flowers. 'Jenny Bloom' produces deep yellow flowers, carried one after another on long, wiry stems. These are bright flowers but not the day-glo hues that send one looking for a pair of sunglasses.

Brightly colored lilies also are effective accents. They bloom for a long time, which is always something to consider in planning a garden. A plant that blooms for only two or three days a year isn't worth the space it takes up in a small garden.

A shady courtyard may call for mostly foliage plants. Some good choices are a collection of ferns; an assortment of hostas (an astounding variety of hostas is available in leaf

A garden statue fits well with this small formal garden. (Photo by Karen Bussolini.)

A fence helps define this garden's structure. (Photo by Karen Bussolini.)

A combination of colors, shapes, and textures makes this porch a welcoming sight. (Photo by Derek Fell.)

colors ranging from yellow to blue, and their lily-like flowers are a real garden pick-me-up in late summer); giant elephant's ear and some impatiens; light-colored coleus; or caladiums for a splash of color.

A hot and sunny bed calls for sun-loving perennials such as daisies and coneflowers, of which there are many choices. Any well-behaved meadow flower will do well here. (Well-behaved means it is not an invasive plant that will choke out everything else, as purple loosestrife is known to do.)

If you have a tiny dooryard garden and not much time to care for it, a sprinkling of pastel impatiens, one of every color you can find, will be a very cheery sight, and with enough water, they will bloom all summer long, right up until frost. Just a couple of potted plants situated at a strategic corner will give your tiny garden an element of height. You may be surprised at the amount of visual interest this will add.

Are you very fond of one color, which you never tire of? Then plant a garden of entirely one color. This is one of my fantasies: blue bulb flowers in the spring, such as Dutch hyacinths, chionodoxa, and English and Spanish bluebells; followed by blue English and German irises, Canterbury bells, and Chinese bellflowers; followed by monkshood, alliums, blue salvia, and delphiniums; and finishing up with those astounding blue *Aster* x *frikartii.* Wow! Or go for a moon garden. Plant tulips, irises, phlox, goatsbeard, astilbes, lilies, and daisies, all in white to reflect the moonlight. They're spectacular!

CONTAINER GARDENS

Your deck, patio, or balcony can reflect these same styles. Try a moon garden on a deck or patio. You'll have a lovely thematic garden of all white flowers in the daytime and an unforgettable experience for cocktails at dusk or a cup of coffee after dinner. Plant moonflower (*Ipomoea noctiflora*) in a big pot with a trellis, and watch this spectacular nocturnal member of the morning-glory family open its 3- to 4-in. white blossoms in about a minute's time at dusk. The process is so fascinating that all unrelated conversation will cease.

You can make a deck or patio into about anything you want, but in general you will want to avoid clutter. Wall-to-wall potted plants around a deck or patio look too crowded and are hard to care for. A much better option for a deck is to hang window boxes from the railings on the outside and fill these with the brightly colored annuals you want to grow that year. This will give you more room on your deck and allow the drainage from watering to go over the side. You can use taller plants such as potted lilies (these

This rooftop garden uses man-made shade to create a varied environment. (Photo by Derek Fell.)

do quite well) and houseplants that you bring outside for summer vacation as your architectural elements for punctuation.

For a patio, you can build large tubs from plans found in any number of garden magazines or purchased from garden centers or mail-order houses. These tubs are available in wood or weatherproof plastic, concrete or terra cotta (a big terra cotta tub is going to cost a bundle of money, though). It's your choice. I prefer wood, but some of the newer plastics have a wood-grain look and are sturdy enough to outlive both you and me. The tubs will give you the much-needed element of height in your garden setting. As well as being a very important part of garden design, height also gives you the feeling of privacy.

ANNUALS AND PERENNIALS

Annual refers to any plant that lives its entire life cycle in a single year, from seed to seed. *Perennial* refers to those plants that go dormant after the growing season and initiate a new cycle of growth during the next year. Perennials produce seeds, but these can be thought of as progeny rather than the reincarnation that occurs with annuals.

Add Annuals to Your Perennial Garden

My garden is basically a perennial garden, but I use a lot of annuals. Most gardens fall into this category, because perennials don't have to be replanted each year. Frankly, the thought of replanting 1,200 sq. ft. every spring would cause me to question the wisdom of the whole enterprise. Perennials are the mainstays that fuel the pleasure of watching the cycle of birth, death, and rebirth each year.

Annuals are very useful in anyone's garden. No perennial plant I know of blooms through three seasons. You can plan for a succession of bloom, but there will always be some bare spots. Annuals are great for filling in those spots with a splash of color. Because annuals live only one growing season, they are in a big hurry to reproduce. Consequently, they produce lots of flowers, which are often intensely colorful to attract pollinators (bees, hummingbirds, and the like). Since annuals tend to be shallow-rooted, you can use them to overplant areas with deeply planted perennial bulbs without disturbing the bulbs.

I have an area devoted to species, or wild, tulips. They are unusual, tiny, colorful, and charming, but they bloom only in spring. By June, a little ripening yellow foliage is all that remains. Would I let this area go to waste for two seasons because I like wild tulips? Certainly not. In June, self-seeding nicotiana, or flowering tobacco, will be germinating, providing green plants for flowering in August. This area mostly takes care of itself; all I have to do is weed occasionally. The perennial wild tulips come back each spring, and the self-seeding nicotiana fills in every summer.

Another late-blooming self-seeder, cleome, performs the same service where I have an early stand of daffodils, followed by Butterfly Lilies in June and July. In the spot where Dutch hyacinths or tulips and puschkinia bloomed in early spring, I overplant with pansies and later petunias. Where there were small fritillaria, I overplant with impatiens. Where English and Spanish bluebells bloomed, an area that later becomes densely shaded, I overplant with impatiens backed up by caladiums.

Architectural elements of pots, trellis, and topiary create visual interest with height and shape. (Photo by Karen Bussolini.)

Try Self-Seeding Annuals

The balanced and harmonious garden will have a place for both annuals and perennials. What are some easy-to-grow annuals? Well, since there's nothing easier than a self-seeding annual, let me again recommend nicotiana and cleome. Pansies and petunias are fine for sunny areas, and impatiens are perfect for shade. Marigolds are great performers, as are salvia and verbena. Ageratum will add a nice blue, alyssum is available in many colors (it's also a champion self-seeder), and strawflowers, besides being brilliantly colored, are easily dried for winter bouquets. A wonderful performer as a self-seeder in Zone 7 and warmer is cosmos. This plant grows up to 5 ft. tall and has light, ferny foliage and brilliantly colored flowers. My favorite variety is 'Bright Lights', which has tones of yellow, amber, red, and brown. *Cosmos astrosanguineus* is a perennial. It is dark reddish brown with a surprising chocolate scent and is hardy through Zone 7. Cosmos can be a spectacular plant, and I certainly recommend that you use it in colder growing zones as well. Just start with new seed. See p. 126 for some catalogs you can peruse for ideas of other self-seeding annuals.

Avoid Extremes

Whichever garden style you pick, try to avoid extremes. Your goal should be to achieve a balanced, pleasing effect and harmony among the plants and their environment. Certainly, more than one kind of harmony exists, and experimenting to find new combinations and juxtapositions to please the eye is fun and commendable. But don't fall into the trap of having to be the first one on your block to grow the new shade of 'Screaming Yellow Yarrow' or those awful celosias, which look like red velvet brains.

Every year, growers invest millions of dollars to come up with new flower varieties. Some are great, such as the tetraploid daylilies with their remarkable color range; some are disquieting, to say the least. Celosia and dianthus now come in some colors that were formerly reserved only for safety clothing worn by highway crews. These plants are not necessarily worth all the time and money it takes to produce them. For example, in the headlong rush to develop new and different varieties, W. Atlee Burpee & Co. offered a $10,000 prize to anyone who could breed a white marigold. Gardeners all over America bent to the task. After years of trying, someone finally succeeded in the late 1970s. Alas, few other companies besides Burpee sell the white marigold anymore. How come? Nobody really wanted white marigolds!

Varied colors and heights give the Calvary Church garden lots of interest in late April.

CHAPTER 3
Prepare Your Garden

ALMOST ANY PATCH OF GROUND you approach with the idea of growing something will need some work, particularly in the city. Generations of builders and demolishers have been scraping away at what passes for soil for so long that often little is left but broken brick, stone, and glass. The soil also may contain many of the by-products of gasoline-powered engines. A couple of years ago, the soil in front of the Calvary Church garden rejected water, which would actually bead up and run off the soil as if the ground had a wax finish. This soil was drastically in need of such amendments as compost and vermiculite. If you actually have some real soil, it's probably been leached poor and compacted. It's up to you to turn it into a growing medium.

WHAT IS GOOD SOIL?

English gardeners, who have soil that has been worked and improved for centuries, say that you should be able to thrust your arm into the soil up to the elbow. Soil like that has good *tilth*—that is, it has everything it needs to nourish great plants. It is dark and rich and very deep. Good tilth is an admirable goal, but not practicable in most urban settings. A more realistic goal is to render your soil to what gardeners call *friable:* crumbly, moisture retentive, and full of good organic material.

**TOOLS YOU WILL NEED
FOR CULTIVATING HARD GROUND**

Some of the necessary tools for cultivating soil you will want to own. Some can be borrowed. Some should be avoided altogether.

TO BUY	TO BORROW	TO NEITHER BUY NOR BORROW
• Spade	• Mattock	• Rototiller
• Garden fork		
• Rake		

CULTIVATING THE SOIL

If your soil is really poor, you may want to add some topsoil. For a small plot, topsoil is available in 50-pound bags from garden centers. For larger plots, a truckload is better. You can often find classified ads in the newspapers for topsoil by the truckload or ton.

Once you spread the topsoil, turn over the soil with your spade to a minimum depth of 12 in.; 16 in. is better. Work the topsoil into the existing soil with a spade or garden fork. Use a mattock (looks like a pickax except that it's flat on one end) to break up stubborn clods. Borrow the mattock from somebody and return it. Don't buy one because you'll probably never need it again. Also, don't buy or rent a rototiller to turn over the soil the first time for hard ground. If you try to use a rototiller on very hard ground, it will almost certainly be ineffectual. Rototillers are designed for churning up previously cultivated ground. They are not intended to be used as earthmoving equipment and often cause injury when they are. (Did you ever wonder why modern science hasn't come up with anything better than a rototiller? We can send spacecraft to the planets, reattach severed limbs, and crack the genetic code. But when it comes to digging up the ground we have this clanking monstrosity that followed the Model T Ford off the assembly line. Why don't we put a team of mechanical engineers on the case and think up something better?)

You should not have to dig out the soil that is there now, unless it is nothing but gravel or asphalt. If small bits of brick or stone remain, they will be good for your soil's drainage. Larger bricks and rocks, however, should be removed. You can use them to make a border or even a rock garden. These days, urban soil also is full of plastics, which will never break down and should be removed.

SOIL AMENDMENTS

You can add several amendments to your soil to improve its quality. Among these are compost, vermiculite, sphagnum moss, earthworms, and fertilizer.

Compost

For organic content, add some compost to your soil. Compost is just decayed organic material, the result of bacterial action and heat. Many cities and towns now offer compost free by the truckload. It comes from decayed leaves the city collected the previous year. Compost also is available in bags from garden centers.

Compost is the most valuable soil additive you can use. It adds beneficial bacteria and nourishing organic matter to the soil, is a great soil conditioner, and retains water. Compost has been called "brown gold," somewhat of a cliché but nonetheless accurate.

If you have enough compost, you can forget about the topsoil for the most part; the majority

of plants would rather grow in compost any day. You also can use compost instead of mulch, and it will add nutrients to your garden year after year.

Turning your own garden waste into "brown gold" is a very attractive proposition. I make some compost myself from plant trimmings and pulled weeds in the very back of the garden in a spot between a crab apple tree and the church wall, where nothing will grow. I make several cubic feet a year and do it more out of a sense of commitment to the environment than anything else. Gardening magazines are full of advertisements for composting equipment.

Don't feel bad if you don't want to go to the trouble of making compost. We are small-space gardeners, you and I. We don't always have enough room to grow all the flowers we want, let alone make piles of compost. So if you have little room, leave the compost-making to the city.

You might be tempted to dig under your old plants and let your compost form right in the soil. This is *not* a good idea. By turning under this raw material, you may be doing more harm than good. During the growing season, plants are hosts to insect eggs, which may thrive underground in the larval stage, producing a new generation the next year. In addition, plants pick up diseases during the growing season, and a winter spent underground may actually nourish the diseases.

By contrast, the normal process of composting is to build a pile of waste material and let bacteria digest it. A by-product of the digestion is heat generated by bacteria in the pile as they break down plant material. This heat destroys insect eggs, weed seeds, and diseases. Just turning the plant material under in your garden does nothing to kill these pests and pestilences. If you want to make doubly sure that no pests get into your compost, burn (if you're allowed to in your neighborhood) or discard any plants with obvious problems.

Vermiculite and Sphagnum Moss

Another way to amend your soil is to add some vermiculite and sphagnum moss for water retention and to make the soil more friable. Vermiculite is a natural form of mica that was blown full of air by a volcanic eruption long ago. It is mined commercially and resembles kitty litter, except that it is lightweight, so you can easily handle bags holding up to several bushels. Any good garden store will have large bags of vermiculite.

This is great stuff and will help any soil indoors or out. It loosens the soil and makes it easier for the roots to grow. It is also excellent to use for cutting commercial potting soil for houseplants. Did you ever notice how the soil in houseplants becomes hard, almost like concrete, after a while? It won't if you cut it with one-third vermiculite.

Vermiculite is better than perlite. Perlite is a commercially made product reminiscent of Styrofoam, which is also used as a soil conditioner. But perlite doesn't hold much water. In addition, it is dead white. It's fine for florist and greenhouse potting mixes, but it is not aesthetically pleasing in garden soil. It looks out of place, something like a fungus.

Sphagnum moss is a natural product obtained from northern peat bogs. It makes the soil lighter and helps it retain water. It also adds organic material to your garden soil. Look for sphagnum moss at a garden center.

Earthworms

Earthworms are soil enhancers. They are inexpensive and commercially available by mail (a few plant catalogs have a listing for them). You don't need to order a lot of earthworms; they will increase rapidly. Their action helps keep the soil loose, and the by-products of their digestion will enrich the soil. Yes, they are wiggly and slimy, but you are an intrepid city gardener. You can do it! Actually, you don't have to touch them at all. You can release them directly into the soil.

Fertilizer

We all want a garden that is "natural" and "organic." It is a noble goal. The reality of the situation, however, is that plants in a garden of mixed annuals and perennials have different feeding needs. There is no one mix of nutrients that will make them all happy. Nasturtiums like very poor soil; fertilize them, and they will become so preoccupied with producing leaves that they won't bloom. Bulb plants need lots of phosphorus to form blossoms and strong stems. It's not a crime against nature to give each group a little of what it needs to perform well. After all, you're not going to eat the flowers (except maybe the nasturtiums or daylilies).

The other side of the coin is that the new gardener often thinks that if some fertilizer is good, more is better. It's not. Most fertilizer is stored chemically as some form of a salt (nitrogen, phosphorus, or potassium) so that it becomes soluble in water and the plants can use it. Too much of these salts in the soil results in chemical burning of the roots, since the fertilizer won't wash out of the soil fast enough to dilute it.

What's the answer? The best solution is good old compost. But some plants will need a little

---

FERTILIZER TIPS

- Check a reference book or the plant tag before you apply fertilizer, to find out what elements a specific plant needs. Read the label on the fertilizer to make sure the needed elements are there.
- Use half the recommended dose to avoid burning by chemical salts.
- Avoid fertilizers with high numbers (such as 45) in the N-P-K formula. These are like fertilizer bombs. A 5-10-5 fertilizer is a much safer combination.

something extra from time to time. One solution is a time-released fertilizer—those little beads that dissolve weeks apart to provide a continuous, uniform feeding over a whole season. I apply this type of fertilizer early in the spring so that the rains have time to wash the nutrients down to the roots before the big growing spurt begins. A couple of pounds is enough for 1,000 sq. ft. If you want to grow nasturtiums, save a spot for them without fertilizer.

Fertilizer formulas are always presented in this way: nitrogen-phosphorus-potassium (N-P-K). Nitrogen produces lush, green growth, phosphorus promotes bloom, and potassium helps build strong stems and roots. This is important to know because you don't want to apply the wrong fertilizer at the wrong time. Lawn specialists apply fertilizer high in nitrogen to produce all those green blades. But when this fertilizer is applied to a flowering plant, it will result in all leaves and no flowers. If applied in the fall, high-nitrogen fertilizer will cause a growth spurt, resulting in winterkill by exposing tender new shoots to freezing weather. In a garden concerned mostly with flowers, you don't need much nitrogen at all.

In the fall and early spring, sprinkle a small amount of a fertilizer high in phosphorus over the spots where you've planted spring bulbs to give them an extra boost. Apply another dose in the spring when they start to emerge, then another when they've finished blooming. Look for a formula of 10-30-10 (10 percent nitrogen, 30 percent phosphorus, and 10 percent potassium) or 5-15-5. If you think a certain plant, such as an azalea or a hydrangea, could use an extra boost during the spring or summer, apply a water-soluble fertilizer such as Miracid. Just remember to use a light touch; half the recommended dose is probably enough.

Phosphorus stimulates flower production. Any purveyor of spring bulbs will be only too glad to sell you a high-phosphorus fertilizer to stimulate flower production of the tulips and daffodils you've just purchased. A liberal application of phosphorus is good for bulbs; but it isn't very smart to order by mail. The freight on a 10-pound bag of fertilizer can be steep. Just zip over to the garden store and get a bag of superphosphate. Put a teaspoon of this in the bottom of the hole where you're going to plant your bulb, cover it with an inch of soil (to prevent burning the bulb's roots), put in the bulb, and cover it with soil. Phosphorus will help the whole garden, not just the bulbs, but it's really necessary for good bulb flower production, particularly those you want to come back for years, such as daffodils, crocuses, and scillas.

Potassium will help make stronger stems to hold up all those wonderful nodding daffodils and tulips. Apply potassium fertilizer over your whole flower garden in the fall and again in the spring. Don't forget to give some to the tall-growing lilies as well. They really need strong stems.

SOIL ACIDITY AND ALKALINITY

It's a good idea to test your soil for acidity or alkalinity. This is important if you want to grow plants that are sensitive to soil, such as hydrangeas, rhododendrons, or azaleas. It's also important in a newly made garden. But there is absolutely no point in doing this before you amend the texture of the soil. Wait until you add all the other stuff to the soil and then see what else it needs.

You can get an inexpensive soil test kit at any garden store or at most hardware stores. The tests are easy to perform, and conditions far outside the norm are easy to correct.

This is a typical fertilizer label, including the N-P-K ratio of 15-30-15.

Ground limestone for lawns will make the soil more alkaline. Aluminum sulfate or a commercial preparation like Miracid will increase acidity. Most plants like it in the neutral zone, between the two extremes. Some plants, such as rhododendrons, just won't perform without the proper acidity. There is a rhododendron beside the church that never bloomed and always looked sickly. After puzzling about this for several years, I concluded that the soil was too alkaline as a result of the rainwater washing off the limestone church. I put two applications of aluminum sulfate around the bush in April, and it bloomed in the middle of May. Hydrangeas also need acid soil. The more acid there is in the soil the more blue (instead of pink) the flower is going to be.

POTTING SOIL FOR CONTAINERS

Almost any standard potting soil is fine as a starting place, but most potting soils will need some amendments, or they will quickly become compacted. Have you ever watered a plant and noticed that the water doesn't sink in? That's most likely because of compaction.

Here's a good formula for potting soil. In a bucket, mix together two parts of commercial potting soil, one part vermiculite, and one part milled sphagnum moss. The vermiculite and sphagnum moss will lighten and aerate the soil and provide both better drainage and better moisture retention.

Good moisture retention is important because you don't want to have to water all those plants every day, and you shouldn't. Plants need to dry out, at least to a certain extent, between waterings. Soil that is always saturated keeps air from getting to the roots, so the roots rot and the plant dies. Whenever someone asks me to look at their "sick" plant, the first sign I look for is overwatering. I am convinced that most container plants die from kindness: overwatered by caring people with the best of intentions.

These ingredients will make a good potting soil (clockwise from the top): 1 part milled sphagnum moss, 2 parts commercial potting soil, and 1 part vermiculite.

Soilless Mixes

If you are starting seeds, use one of the soilless mixes designed for this purpose. They're free of weed seeds, insects, and soil diseases. They're also resistant to mold, which is important in starting seeds. A disease known as damping-off can easily invade seedbeds. It attacks the base of the stem of an emerging plant and weakens it so that the little plant falls over and dies. The soilless mixes will retard damping-off. If you do see a little white fuzz appearing in your seed trays, soak the whole tray in a solution of benomyl or Benlate, two antifungal preparations.

A number of soilless mixes are available. I recommend Park's Grow Mix, marketed by Park Seed Co. (see p. 127).

A surprisingly good garden arrangement for a public space, composed by The New York City Parks and Recreation Department.

CHAPTER 4
Mulch

EARLY SUMMER is the time of year when mulch will begin to show its obvious value by suppressing weeds and retaining soil moisture. There are more kinds of mulch than Carter had little liver pills, as the saying goes. Almost anything, from newspaper, black plastic, and gravel to shredded bark, peanut shells, and grass clippings, can be considered mulch.

WHAT IS MULCH?

Mulch is any kind of cover for the garden soil. Mulch retards the growth of weeds and controls the temperature and moisture content of the soil. It can be any substance that won't of its own accord take root and grow. Mulch will save you a lot of time and effort and keep your plants healthy.

Mulch reduces water evaporation from the soil, meaning you have to water less. It helps the ground absorb rainfall without runoff and keeps the soil cooler. It also reduces splashing from rain falling on bare soil and so keeps the plant leaves cleaner. It helps your garden appear well groomed.

Farmers like black plastic mulch because absolutely *no* weeds will grow through it and because the black absorbs heat and makes young plants grow faster. It is, however, unattractive, and you wouldn't want it around your flowers. Gravel will keep down weeds, but it also will mix with the soil. Soon every time you stick in a trowel, you'll be hitting rocks. Neither of these mulches will do anything to improve the soil itself.

One word of caution: Don't use mulch where you want plants to self-seed. Just as mulch keeps weeds from germinating, it also does so with flower seeds.

ORGANIC MULCHES

The benefits of organic mulches are that they break down and become part of the soil, improving and conditioning it, and they keep soil temperatures more uniform in winter. I recommend organic mulches such as bark chips, cocoa bean hulls, compost, and manure.

Newspaper
Newspaper is very efficient at suppressing weeds, but it does have several drawbacks. First, you need some space to lay out sheets of newspaper. This is easy between tomato plants but difficult among daylilies. Second, it is ugly, which sort of defeats the purpose as far as flower gardens go. If you use newspaper, you will want to cover it with a layer of something else. You also should punch some holes in it to let rainfall through. Newspaper without holes

Shredded cedar bark mulch—fresh to the right, aged to the left—looks natural.

will hold moisture in, but it also will cause rainwater to run off. Stay away from the color sections in food gardens as they contain toxic substances.

Shredded Bark

Shredded bark is a good choice because it looks very natural. Try shredded cedar bark. It's a nice dark brown when it goes on, and it ages to a dark, weathered gray just like a cedar house. It is not expensive and is easy to apply. In a couple of years, it will become part of your garden soil. As it decays, it adds humus, partially decayed vegetable matter that gives good garden soil its texture, water-retention abilities, and drainage potential.

Bark Chips

Bark chips are typically pine and are ground to about an inch square. They make the most efficient organic mulch because weeds have a devil of a time taking root in them—a very good quality in a mulch. If you want something permanent, to put around evergreens or other trees, for instance, you can't beat bark chips. It will be

many a year before they decay, though, so if you want mulch to add organic matter to the soil, make another choice.

Shells and Hulls

Shells and hulls make an attractive mulch. Use pecan shells, peanut shells, beechnut hulls . . . any manner of nut or bean shell. My mother always used cocoa bean hulls. The chocolate smell hung around for weeks. Shells and hulls are efficient and provide good water absorption. They are *not* a good choice, however, if you live in an especially windy area because they are lightweight and tend to blow away.

Compost

Good old compost! A thick layer of compost will suppress weeds and add natural organic fertilizer to your soil. Compost is still the best mulch you can get. If you don't have a compost pile of your own, many cities and towns turn collected leaves into compost and give it away. Get some!

Manure

How many times have I read, "Now add some well-rotted manure." Right! Where are small-space gardeners like you and me going to find a big pile of well-rotted manure that we can carry off to our gardens? (If you happen to find one, let me know!) You can get desiccated cow manure by the bag at garden stores, but it is prohibitively expensive to use as a deep mulch. Also, even the "deodorized" kind will stink for a few days when it gets wet. If you do use manure, add it in the fall. Don't use manure around peonies—they don't like it.

Grass Clippings, Leaves, and the Like

Grass clippings make a good mulch that is high in nitrogen. Since there's usually no shortage of grass clippings except in the most urban environments, this is a cheap source of mulch. Grass clippings heat up when they rot, so keep them a few inches away from plant stems. You also will do well to poke some holes through the clippings as they flatten out. Grass clippings can form a dense mat that will keep rainwater out if you don't provide channels descending into the soil.

You also can use shredded leaves, ground corncobs, pine needles, straw, and many other things I haven't mentioned as mulch. Just be sure that what you choose isn't a fire hazard, hasn't been treated with chemicals that might harm your plants, and doesn't detract from your garden's beauty.

SOIL POLYMER "MULCH" FOR CONTAINERS

As mentioned, one of the admirable qualities of any mulch is its water-retention abilities. A soil polymer will do this for your patio plants, much to their benefit. It's a soil additive that will absorb 400 times its weight in water. Several brands are available, marketed under names such as HydroSource or SoilMoist.

This is how you use it: Put a couple of tablespoons of either of these products in a 3-gallon bucket and fill the bucket with water. In about 15 minutes, the polymer will have absorbed most of the water and swollen to fill the bucket. If we're going to be away for a week or so, we spread this over the soil in each pot to a depth of about 1 in. The polymer slowly releases water, and when we return, the houseplants are in great shape.

Caution: A couple of tablespoons of these crystals in a bucket looks mighty meager, and you'll be tempted to add more. Don't, or you'll have this stuff all over your floor, and it's very slippery and hard to pick up.

Polymer crystals were never designed to be mulch, but they play the role admirably.

Spots of seasonal color draw the eye around the garden. (Photo by Brian Coats.)

CHAPTER 5
Essential Tools

"EVERY WORKMAN NEEDS A GOOD TOOL." Who said that? I can't remember, but it's true! You're going to need more than one good tool, and here are the basics required for any garden, regardless of its size.

SPADE

A spade is a digging tool with an almost flat blade about 12 in. long and 8 in. wide. It has a long handle and foot treads on top of the blade so that you can push it into the soil. Overall a spade measures 40 to 42 in. A spade is not a shovel. A shovel is a scoop with a long handle that is used for throwing coal into a vintage furnace or mucking out a stable. A spade has much nobler ends—namely, planting beautiful flowers and trees in your garden. You will use the spade for those really big jobs when you are getting started and less frequently later. However, it will always be an important tool in your garden. Therefore, do not scrimp and buy a cheap one. Buy a better one made of good steel and take care of it. Get a file to sharpen it, a brush to clean it, and some machine oil to keep it from rusting. Or get a bucket, fill it with sand, and pour in a couple of quarts of motor oil. Each time you use your spade (or other tool), stick it in this sand-oil mixture. It will clean the spade and keep it oiled.

GARDEN FORK

A garden fork has much the same uses as a spade. Instead of the slightly curved blade, it has four long tines. These tines slip into the soil much more easily than a flat blade, so this tool is very useful for turning over large areas of earth—something you will be doing a lot of in the beginning but also on occasion later on, such as when you want to plant a large number of tulips. A fork also is useful for adding soil amendments such as sphagnum moss to the soil and mixing it in. Buy a good fork and treat it like the spade.

RAKE

This isn't one of those springy leaf rakes; this is a garden rake. Solid steel on a long handle. You will have considerable use for this when you get started and only occasional use for it later, so buy the bargain version and forget about it. It will last a while, if you keep it clean.

Spades, a garden fork, and a good rake are essential tools.

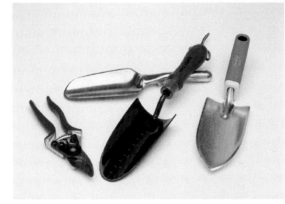

Look for tools of good quality that won't hurt your hands.

TROWEL

A trowel is like a little spade. You will use it to excavate small holes for some bulbs and to set out individual plants whenever you acquire them. It's good to have two sizes, a wide one and a narrow one, because one size is not always appropriate. Even the best trowels won't break the bank, so be advised that really cheap ones tend to bend.

DIBBLE

A dibble is an adaptation of the most primitive of planting tools, the pointed stick. It is 10 or 11 in. long, sometimes with a transverse handle on top. Its business end is sharpened to a point and sheathed in metal. You use this tool for planting small bulbs and plants. A good dibble is hard to find in stores, but many catalogs offer this tool (see p. 126).

GARDEN SHEARS OR CLIPPERS

These are scissors made for the garden. Regular household scissors will rust away or become terminally disabled in the garden very quickly, but good shears or clippers will last for years if properly cared for. Shears or clippers also are items worth spending some money on. You will regret buying cheap ones because they won't do the job, they'll hurt your hand, or both. Catalogs (see p. 126) offer some fine shears and clippers that are generally better than those you can find in stores.

PRUNERS

Essentially a pair of scissors, pruners have a heavy cutting blade for pruning thicker branches than your clippers will cut through. (If you don't use pruners, you will soon ruin your clippers.) Be sure to buy the bypass (scissor) type, not the anvil type. The Swiss-made Felco pruners are the best and even come in right- and left-handed models.

Good watering cans, gloves, and a dibble are worth the investment.

WATERING CAN

Yes, you have a hose, but do you want to drag out a hose to water a couple of potted plants or a tiny little planting of violas? Of course not! You need a watering can. Galvanized steel cans with a genuine brass rose (that's the sprinkler head) look great, but they cost a fortune and are heavy. Get a lightweight plastic one instead. Gardener's Supply Company (see p. 129) has a great one. It's light, holds 3 gallons, and will last your entire lifetime.

GLOVES

Gloves are essential if you care about avoiding injury or how your hands look. Get a good pair of horsehide gloves that will protect your hands from thorns and blisters. Gloves also will keep your hands clean. Some garden tasks, such as planting small bulbs, require more tactile sense than horsehide gloves will allow. The perfect gloves for these operations are those disposable latex gloves that dentists and doctors wear for examinations. They are available at drugstores and hardware stores and will not only let you feel what you're doing but also help keep your nails clean.

The combined textures of stucco wall, trellis, and gnarled tree are the "spine" for the flowering plants. (Photo by Karen Bussolini.)

CHAPTER 6
Composition in the Garden

COMPOSITION IS THE PLACEMENT of shapes, textures, and colors that will draw the eye into a picture. The soul of composition is the triangle. If you look at great paintings and photographs, you will see that most, if not all, are full of triangular shapes. Portrait painters place their subjects to one side of the canvas to create a triangular shape, and this serves to transport the eye toward the face.

The same principle applies to the garden. As you are thinking about how to lay out your space, look for triangles from the primary point of view—that is, from where you think they will be seen the most. This may not be obvious unless you have a background (like mine, which is the church wall) that dictates where the planting known as the key should be placed. If not, draw your dream garden from ground-level perspective. I think the perspective is much more informative than the conventional overhead view. You'll never see your garden from overhead unless you're flying in an airplane. First draw your key. Now draw a line from the top of the key to each end of your garden to form the two sides of the triangle. The ground level forms the hypotenuse.

Varying the height of your plantings will give your garden its three dimensions, just as vary-ing levels makes rooms inside a house more interesting. It will also help you to create those "rooms" full of surprises.

THE KEY

Every garden should have an anchor, a key plant that acts as the hub around which the garden revolves. Even if you have just a small space, I urge you to consider devoting some of it to a tree or tall shrub. It will give your growing space depth and sophistication of design. If you have a larger space, you might consider secondary keys as well.

Key Plantings

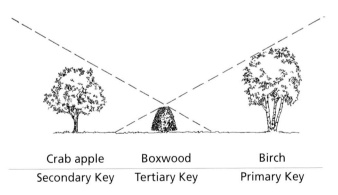

Crab apple	Boxwood	Birch
Secondary Key	Tertiary Key	Primary Key

Triangulation is the guiding principle in the placement of the key plantings in the Calvary Church garden. The larger keys create a frame for the overall "painting."

A refreshing terrace oasis above city streets. (Photo by Karen Bussolini.)

Even though the key plant will be the hub, you do not necessarily have to place it smack-dab in the center of the garden. It might make for a better composition to place it to one side or the other, depending on what architectural elements are involved (house, wall, fence, and so on). You don't have to put it in the back just because it is tall. Placing it somewhat forward will help create a feeling of depth.

Secondary Plantings

From your key plant, move on to your foundation plantings. These are the secondary perennial plants that will be your garden's skeleton or structural support and will largely determine its shape for years to come. They will likely be shrubs or small trees, even a vine growing on a trellis. I consider my *small* birch tree (I prune it to keep it that way) to be my key plant. The crab apple and boxwood are secondary but very important to the three-dimensional shape.

Another technique to create depth is the repetition of shapes or colors receding down your garden path. For example, place two veronica plants on opposite sides of your path. Place another two plants 4 or 5 ft. farther on, and a third set at the same distance. The effect of this planting will be to draw the eye down the walk, creating much the same effect as columns.

A climbing rose makes a great floral backdrop for lower plants.

This courtyard makes maximum use of space for flowers. (Photo by Karen Bussolini.)

SELECTING THE KEY

Your anchor plant can be of any size that fits your garden's scale, but it is very important to choose one that will be complementary to the other plantings and is suitable for your climate. For instance, you would not want to plant a southern magnolia if you lived in Vermont. It would only die, and you'd have to start over. This is true with many of the horticultural oddities you see in catalogs. If you've never heard of a plant before, it might be because it doesn't grow well where you live.

It is much wiser to select a plant that is native to your area or that grows in very similar conditions. For instance, if you see a dogwood tree growing wild in the woods near your home, it might be a good choice for a small tree in your garden. Witch hazel is a good choice for the Northeast because it thrives in the wild there. Consult the USDA Plant Hardiness Zone Map on p. 131 to help you with your selection.

Do not choose anything that is invasive or that produces obnoxious fruit. By invasive I mean trees such as the willow, which grows fast and has long, strangling roots. Willows have been known to break sewer and water pipes within their clutches. Someone once gave me some rooted pussy willow branches to plant in the garden, which I didn't, because I could envision them with a death grip on the subway tunnels under Park Avenue South.

One tree with obnoxious fruit is the Osage orange, which produces grapefruit-size green balls that drop off and rot. Another tree to avoid is the female ginkgo tree, which produces thousands of small green fruits that squish underfoot and exude the odor of putrid meat. The fruit of the mulberry tree stains clothing and attracts so many birds that it becomes a problem.

Following are some suggestions for effective key plants:

• **European white birch.** This is an attractive and well-behaved tree. In addition to its small green summer leaves, its white-and-black bark and multiple trunks give it winter interest. You can prune this tree to keep down its size; it

A flowering cherry combines great color with an attractive shape. (Photo by Charles Mann.)

won't mind at all. A birch will do just fine in a container in your roof garden, too.

• **Flowering crab apple.** Although this tree does produce fruit, the fruit is not messy in summer and looks very nice in the fall when the little apples turn red. In spring, the tree is covered with white or pink flowers. This tree, too, can be pruned to keep its size manageable.

• **Flowering cherry or plum.** These are both members of the genus *Prunus*. They, too, produce fruits following the white or pink flowers, but the little fruits are not a problem. Many species will attain a wide side growth but not become very tall, which gives them a very pleasing shape.

• **Dogwood.** Dogwoods are hardy from Zone 5 all the way down into Florida. They are attractive little trees with large white, pink, or red

A small American dogwood softens the line of this iron gate.

A Japanese maple is a great accent plant in almost any style garden. (Photo by Charles Mann.)

cruciform blossoms in spring and attractive red berries in fall. The dogwood blooms before leafing out. The leaves turn pleasing shades of red and orange in the fall.

There is also an oriental dogwood (*Cornus kousa chinensis*), which blooms into June and July, after it leafs out. It makes a very attractive planting, with the leaves forming a nice background for the profuse white blooms. Its ultimate growth will be taller than its American counterpart, so take that into consideration.

• **Japanese maple.** This is among the loveliest and most desirable of all trees. It has eye-catching red or green leaves that are often deeply cut and lacy. Many varieties are available. Some do not grow above 6 ft., so they fit in with a small plot or a roof or patio garden just fine. Some varieties have bark that is tinted with coral for added winter interest. These trees are very malleable and can be pruned to any shape. They can be treated much like bonsai and lend themselves very well to the gnarled shape so loved by the Japanese. You will never tire of this tree.

• **Witch hazel.** Witch hazel is a remarkable plant. *Hamamelis vernalis* will burst into bloom during a warm spell in the middle of winter. And I have seen *H. virginiana* blooming at the end of November in Essex, Connecticut, where most of the world's supply of witch hazel solution is distilled.

Witch hazel produces fragrant, feathery, yellow or coppery red flowers when nothing else is

Witch hazels provide very early spring color interest. (Photo by Charles Mann.)

blooming, so it is a welcome sight. Thickets of witch hazel grow up to 20 ft. in height but can be pruned to a lower level. It is a very hardy woodland plant that will survive temperatures of −20° F and below.

If you happen to be in a thicket of witch hazel in spring, you may be startled by a popping sound or struck by little missiles. These are witch hazel seeds. To get the seeds far enough away from the parent plant, witch hazel has evolved a ballistic technique. The seed cases burst open with such force that they often propel the seeds up to 20 ft. away.

• **Callery pear.** This tree is in much demand in urban areas because it is drought, heat, and pollution tolerant. It does just fine on my busy street corner, which is often hot, dry, and polluted (or frigid, wet, and polluted). Masses of small white flowers appear in spring, making this shapely 18- to 20-ft. tree a real attraction. It does have fruit—little reddish brown pears about half an inch long—but you will probably never notice them.

• **Lilac.** If you have good sun, try a lilac. Lilacs are beautiful plants, and the blossoms exude one of the most enchanting fragrances in the world. Lilacs are now available in many colors, including yellow, white, pink, and deep purple, in addition to the traditional light purple, or lilac

The callery pear is a reliable tree in urban environments.

Lilacs bring old-fashioned charm, but need lots of sun to perform. (Photo by Charles Mann.)

The mugo pine, a Japanese favorite, is a long-lived, small tree that thrives on neglect. (Photo by Charles Mann.)

color. Lilacs do not like overly acid or alkaline soil (pH), so they won't be happy with azaleas or hydrangeas. (See Chapter 3 for an explanation of pH.) A lilac should do fine on your roof.

• **Small evergreens.** The smaller evergreens, such as the mugo pine, are good choices as keys for a patio or rooftop. The mugo pine is especially adaptable to containers, tolerates a wide variety of conditions, and has no pests to speak of. Most other small evergreens are also essentially pest-free and so are good candidates for growing in a tub. (I have seen some minor scale invasions on container-planted evergreens, but this is easily remedied with an oil-based spray.)

PLANTING THE KEY IN THE GROUND

There are just a few basics for planting these trees. Dig a hole as deep as the rootball and a foot wider in diameter. Loosen the soil at the bottom of the hole to allow the roots some freedom to grow. If the tree is in a container, lift it out and set it in the hole. If it is wrapped in burlap, set the whole thing in the hole and loosen the burlap from the sides. Leave the burlap underneath the rootball. Burlap is biodegradable, and the roots will grow right through it.

Fill the hole up to the top of the rootball, then tamp down the soil with your foot. Where it sinks, fill in with more soil and tamp again. Do not heap soil around the trunk or bury it any deeper than it has been growing. Adequate oxygen must be allowed to reach the roots and thus prevent the trunk from rotting and being exposed to soil pests. After the tree has been planted, water it generously.

PLANTING THE KEY IN A CONTAINER

Planting a tree in a container is really no different. Make sure you have 6 to 8 in. of soil or growing medium underneath the rootball and a similar amount on the sides. You will not want this tree to grow into a mighty forest denizen on your patio, so don't give it too much room in the container. Do not plant the trunk deeper than the top of its rootball, or the trunk may rot. That will mean curtains for your little tree.

Feed Your Tree

I think people have a tendency to treat trees as architecture, a type of living column that we don't have to care for at all. In fact, most trees don't need us, for anything. But once you put a tree in a pot, it's just another potted plant and needs your attention. A little basic plant food in liquid form in the spring is good for a small tree, and a light pruning late in the fall will help it to keep its shape.

Provide Drainage

It is absolutely essential for a potted tree to have good drainage. If you check the tree after a rainfall and the container is full of standing water, your tree's not going to be with you for long. So before you plant it, drill extra holes in the bottom of the tub or pot. Put some *plastic* mesh in the bottom (metal will quickly decay)

to keep the other ingredients from washing out. Then put in several inches of gravel to assist with the drainage, and plant the tree. Providing good drainage now will save you a great deal of work later on.

Think about Moving

Unless you plan to stay where you live for many years, it is prudent to think about how you will move the tree when you move, or you may need to bring in a crane to do the job. Placing appliance rollers or other rollers made specifically for plant containers under the pot or tub will solve the problem. They will support a great deal of weight, so you'll be able to move your tree to different parts of your deck or patio should you want to rearrange. And when it comes time for the big move, you can roll your tree right into the moving van.

CARING FOR THE KEY

If you wish to prune your key plant in succeeding years, cut off the offending branches at the base, flush with the supporting trunk. Don't leave the stub of a limb, as this provides an entry point for boring insects or diseases. Let the cut heal naturally. Tree sealants actually retard healing and can turn cuts into sites hospitable to infections or abscesses.

Feed trees with a balanced fertilizer in the spring. Fall feeding can cause a spurt of growth that will be killed by the first frost. If you have chosen an evergreen plant, water it during winter warm spells. Cold winds are very drying to evergreens, especially newly planted ones.

The curving line of the plantings reflects the randomness in nature. (Photo by Mick Hales.)

CHAPTER 7

Your Point of View

HOW YOU WANT YOUR GARDEN to be viewed has much to do with how you plant it. Basically, you can view a garden in three ways: from outside, from inside, or both. A garden to be seen from outside will almost always have a more limited perspective and therefore needs to be more disciplined or structured in arrangement. (Yes, there are exceptions, but by and large the rule holds true.) This is because the possible points of view are limited. (Point of view refers to your garden's audience, not you. You can view it from the middle of the lilies if you want.) Using my garden as an example, the points of view are limited to 180 degrees, or two sides. The other 180 degrees is a brownstone wall. This means that much of my garden has to be planted in ascending order of height—the shortest plants in the front, the tallest in the back—for them all to be seen. This is the general rule for most gardens. Although your plants should not be arrayed like soldiers on a field, height is very important.

SURPRISE, SURPRISE

A garden, large or small, should invite you in. It should have perspective and mystery: *What is that splash of color just around the corner? What will I see if I go two steps farther in?* We're not talking about really big vistas here, just some surprises created by the architectural elements of plants and trees, even knee-high plants. This is quite possible in a small garden. In a sense, the garden becomes a series of rooms. Even if you have just one tiny garden path, think of all the side rooms that are possible off this path. You don't have to be able to walk into the rooms, just look into them. They can be as small as 2 ft. by 2 ft.!

ELEMENTS OF YOUR DESIGN

Site your garden where it and its many rooms will be the focal point of the locale. Mine works fine because it's against the brownstone wall of the church and is unique to its location: The other three corners of the intersection are occupied by large buildings. Your garden should not have to compete with its environs, so try to find a spot that is sheltered from grand vistas. A garden planted in front of a breathtaking view of the mountains will not be seen. If you live in Colorado, plant your garden away from the surrounding mountain views.

Another element of garden design is the curved line. Nature never does anything in a straight line. That's why gardens of straight-line beds look more like the work of a surveyor than a gardener. The curved and recurved line is much more pleasing to the eye. If you plan a curved pathway, it will add mystery because your plan and plantings will not all be completely obvious. The viewer will need to make the journey down the path to look into all the rooms. (Even if you are the only viewer on a given day, this is still loads of fun.)

The elements in a garden also should vary in height. Breaking up the planes will make your flower garden seem much more natural and will add punctuation. I have a 6-ft. boxwood right in the middle of my summer perennials. It does wonders to relieve the sameness of 300 black-eyed Susans.

In a small plot, it is better not to think in terms of beds. You will be better served by planning a walkway or pathway surrounded by plants, a curved line to let you add new perspectives. Why should you confine your flowers to beds? Better to confine the people to the walkway. You don't need to plant this with grass. Grass is a lot of trouble. You have to mow it, it doesn't bloom, it doesn't provide food, and it will most certainly overgrow its boundaries and try to choke out your flowers. Use bricks, wood chips, slate, flagstone, or anything else that will keep your feet dry after a rain and won't multiply.

Plant Height and Point of View

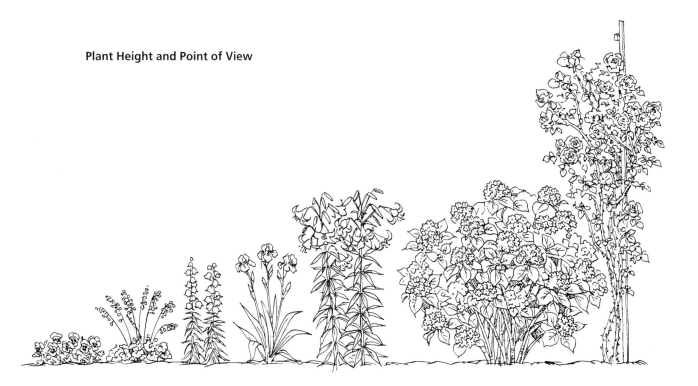

You don't need to line up your garden plants with military precision, but some thought to their eventual height when you are planting will help them to be seen to their best advantage.

The geometric echo of the stones in the design of the bed draws the eye to the daffodils. (Photo by Karen Bussolini.)

THE PLOT THICKENS

The succeeding chapters provide examples of how you might plant a small garden for nine months of bloom. The plants I've included are hardy to Zone 6. (To find out what growing zone you're in, check the USDA Plant Hardiness Zone Map on p. 131.) I have chosen Zone 6 because it's more or less the average. Most of my suggestions also will work for Zones 4, 5, 7, and 8. If you live in Zone 9 or 10, consult a book on desert or tropical gardening. And Zone 3 is too cold for most of these plants; try a book on Alpine gardening. In Zones 1 or 2, try tundra plants. Regardless of the zone you live in, you can create a wonderful small garden using the plants that are hardy in your area.

CHAPTER 8

The Spring Openers: March through April

AFTER THREE OR FOUR MONTHS of watching the garden huddled in its winter blacks, browns, and grays or wondering what's going on under all that snow, most gardeners are on the prowl in February and March, searching the ground for a sign of anything green. When we do find the first shoot, it's a big occasion. We run inside to tell our mates about this great event. They look at us as if we're deranged. And thus starts another year of gardening.

BULBS, CORMS, AND TUBERS

A significant aspect of the spring garden, of course, is the welcome color of flowering bulbs. In fact the word "bulb" is often misused to encompass all plants not grown from seed. A brief explanation of the differences among bulbs, corms, and tubers is in order.

For the sake of definition, a bulb already contains fully formed leaves and flowers in the embryonic stage when you plant it. Lilies and daffodils are bulbs. Lily bulbs are covered with scales, or embryonic leaves (be careful not to knock them off in planting). Bulb stems arise from the base of the bulb. Onions are also bulbs and a lot cheaper than lilies. If you want to see what's inside a bulb, cut open an onion from top to bottom.

Corms are shaped like bulbs, but the embryonic leaves are inside, and the stem and flower, which are fully formed in miniature, arise from the top of the corm. A corm is a storehouse of starch. The plant will use the corm as food and, after flowering, will produce another. Tulips are corms.

A tuber is a starchy food repository. Unlike the corm, the tuber will continue to grow. The leaves and stems grow from "eyes," as in the dahlia or the potato. If you want to see what's inside your dahlia tubers, cut open a potato.

Bulbs, corms, and tubers are all the storehouse stage of the resulting plant. Like any storehouse of food, they need to be kept at ideal temperatures and moisture levels, which for virtually all spring bulbs means refrigeration for 8 to 12 weeks before planting.

SUGGESTED PLANTINGS	
TALLEST	Forsythia
TALLER	Large daffodils, Virginia bluebells
MEDIUM HEIGHT	Narcissus, jonquils
FAIRLY SHORT	Miniature daffodils, Dutch hyacinths
SHORT	Snowdrops, crocuses, puschkinia, chionodoxa, scilla

THE GARDEN IN SPRING

A Solomon's-seal

B Ferns

C *Helleborus orientalis*

D Tulips

E Daffodils

F Rhododendron

G Snowdrops/scilla

H Crocus

I Climbing rose

J *Fritillaria imperialis*

K Bleeding heart

L Boxwood (evergreen)

M Daffodils with muscari

N Erythronium

O Spanish bluebells

P Violets

Q Chionodoxa

R Dicentra

S Small allium

T Species tulips

U Ivy

V Tulips with puschkinia

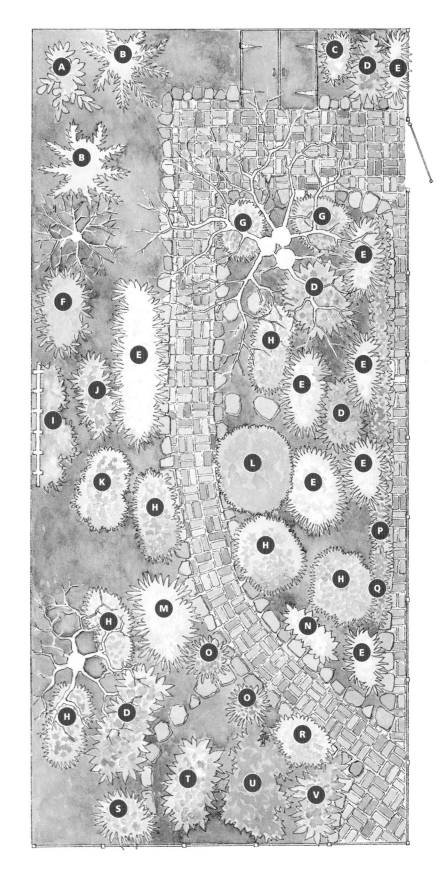

Many of Grandmother's favorites line this walk in early spring. (Photo by Karen Bussolini.)

Snowdrops and winter aconite are first to appear in spring. (Photo by Mick Hales.)

SMALL BULBS

I recommend using your dibble to poke down in the soil just deep enough to plant snowdrops and other small bulbs. Make the hole wide enough to assure that the bulb goes in with the right side up. When you plant any bulb, make sure to plant it with the root end down. Generally, you can see where the roots grow. Also, the pointed end is usually the top. With smaller bulbs and corms, this might not be obvious, so exercise some care. Plant early in the fall rather than late. This gives the bulbs time to get established and grow some roots before winter gets a grip on us.

You can use these small, early bulbs in just about any light. Full sun is no problem for them, and the garden that is shady in summer isn't shady yet. These bulbs will have enough time to manufacture food before the trees shade them fully.

Snowdrops

First to appear will be the snowdrops (*Galanthus nivalis*), around the first of March or maybe even in February. These are little, white, down-facing flowers that nod in the slightest breeze but are remarkably hardy. They often push their way up through several inches of snow. They need to be planted in large numbers to be effective because they are so small. One or two look rather pitiful. They like soil with a lot of humus, and, like most bulbs, they don't like wet feet. If planted in a spot with good drainage, they will reward you by reappearing year after year. Plant them in the fall, 4 or 5 in. deep.

Crocuses

The crocuses will follow about two weeks later. Crocuses look great in groups of all the same color or mixed. Your preference is your only guide. Try them both ways. I prefer large groups of the same color. Crocuses will do fine in sun or open shade. At this time of year, there are no leaves to speak of on deciduous trees and shrubs, so that means crocuses will do well almost anywhere. They also are not particularly choosy about soil. Many people plant them in lawns. They bloom so early that the lawn mower isn't a threat to their leaves, which need to make food for the bulb before they retire for the season. Like almost any plant, however, they do best in humus-rich garden soil. Use a dibble to plant them about 5 in. deep.

Puschkinia

Puschkinia libanotica, named for a Russian botanist, has upright stems of tiny, cup-shaped white flowers with blue accents. Close up, the flowers have the coloring of fine Japanese porcelain. They are great planted in a tight grouping. Since the flowers last a long time, I like them for an underplanting to soften the formality of later-blooming Dutch hyacinths or tulips. Puschkinia is not common in the United States, so you will probably be the only person on your block to grow it. Plant the bulbs 4 to 5 in. deep.

Chionodoxa

Chionodoxa has tiny blue stars with white centers and looks very nice mixed with puschkinia. Alternatively, chionodoxa looks great in a group by itself. This tiny Turkish native is also good as an underplanting for larger bulbs, such as Dutch hyacinths, or around the feet of the

Chionodoxa makes a foil to early daffodils.

earlier-blooming varieties of yellow or white narcissus. This is a wonderful effect, and I highly recommend that you try it.

Scilla

The single, tiny blue flowers of *Scilla siberica* are lovely in a group off by themselves. They are very blue indeed. They also are very early, following right on the heels of the snowdrops. Because they're so tiny, you need to plant a lot of bulbs or you won't really notice the flowers. About a hundred bulbs planted 5 in. deep makes a nice show in the spring. One hundred bulbs sounds like a lot, but you can dig a large

'Queen of the Blues' crocus looks great in clusters.

Prussian-blue *Scilla siberica* is a self-seeder. (Photo by Paddy Wales.)

hole and plant them all at once, or dig several holes with 10 to 20 bulbs. Scilla spreads well, so soon you'll have lots.

Miniature Daffodils

By mid-April, miniature daffodils should be in full bloom. Miniature daffodils are just like the bigger ones except they're 6 to 12 in. tall. There are many fine varieties such as *Narcissus canaliculatus* (a hardy *N. tazetta*). Its blooms stand only 6 in. high, but it looks just like its larger cousins. Miniature daffodils are great for odd corners where you don't have anything else. Or you can plant them next to chionodoxa or scilla. You also can tuck miniature daffodils into a rock garden, in a gap between paving stones, or anyplace else where an extra spot of cheeriness will help brighten things up.

'Jack Snipe' is a hardy 8-in. miniature that is white with a clear yellow cup. For something really unusual, try *N. bulbocodium conspicuus,* or hoop-petticoat. This tiny charmer is virtually all center cup, giving it the look of a small yellow megaphone. It stands 6 to 8 in. tall.

Dutch hyacinths are the husky members of the large-bulb clan. (Photo by Janet Loughrey.)

All of these little guys should be planted 6 to 8 in. deep. Get out the trowel because the dibble won't do it.

LARGER BULBS

The larger bulbs discussed below generally are planted at about 8 in., deeper than the smaller bulbs. I have known people who believe in planting daffodils as much as 16 in. deep as a protective measure, but over the long haul the bloom is not very satisfactory.

Dutch Hyacinths

By the beginning of April, the Dutch hyacinths should be starting their yearly show. Dutch hyacinths are the product of hundreds of years of plant breeding. They are native to the eastern end of the Mediterranean Sea, but no one there would recognize them now. They have become big, husky bulbs that bloom with no more nourishment than water, and they have a magnificent perfume.

I like to underplant hyacinths with something small, like puschkinia or early pansies, which de-emphasizes their formality. Hyacinths come in many colors: The blues are more formal and subdued, and the pinks and yellows are livelier. Hyacinths appreciate lots of sun and a well-drained spot where they can be planted 6 to 8 in. deep.

Large Daffodils

Daffodils, narcissus, and jonquils are all from the same genus. In common parlance, daffodils are narcissus with large, wide "cups"—the central petals of the flower that form what looks like a cup. Narcissus are those with shorter, less prominent cups, and jonquils are those with very short cups. Members of the narcissus family are the most familiar spring flowers. Many are very fragrant, and you will often catch their perfume from 10 ft. away. I will not presume to tell you which varieties to try—there are so many lovely ones.

Narcissus look best planted in groups in the garden or in drifts around trees or fences. The way to space them out in the yard is to put the

bulbs in a basket and toss them into one area, then plant them where they land. Just remember when choosing a planting site that you'll have to allow the foliage to mature after the blooms fade. That's what builds up food in the bulb for next year's bloom. This foliage will turn yellow and become somewhat unsightly before it's completely gone, so it's a good idea to interplant narcissus with later-blooming plants or to plant them at the edge of a larger flowering shrub. Try interplanting them with some early lilies, such as the Butterfly Lily collection from White Flower Farm (see p. 128). I am extremely pleased with the effect this creates in my garden.

Varieties have a wide range of bloom time, April through May, so take this into consideration when selecting yours. It is very nice to have a succession of bloom, so you will want a selection of early, middle, and late bloomers to take up the whole season.

All the narcissus like to be planted 8 to 10 in. deep. In the yard, use your big trowel. In the garden, it will be easier to excavate the planting site with your garden fork. Sprinkle some high-phosphorus fertilizer in the hole and cover it with an inch of soil. Then put in the bulbs and cover with soil. This makes the phosphorus available to the bulbs without burning from the phosphate salts.

Virginia Bluebells

What looks nice with daffodils? It's not a bulb, but the classic backup planting for narcissus and tulips is Virginia bluebells (*Mertensia virginica*). These are nothing like Spanish or English bluebells. The 18-in. herbaceous plant produces clusters of bluish blossoms that nod in the spring wind. These blue clusters are the perfect complement to the yellow and cream of daffodils or to a group of red tulips.

Virginia bluebells are native to the borders of woods. Consequently, they like semishade, moisture, and a humus-rich, slightly acid soil—pretty much what narcissus like. So if you plant your narcissus near a shady spot, plant Virginia bluebells just behind them. By midsummer bluebells die back completely, so make sure to

Virginia bluebells help to soften the loud statement of red tulips.

Tiny alliums make good partners for bluebells and ferns. (Photo by Mick Hales.)

mark the spot so that you don't accidentally disturb their rest period. This plant has no pests.

Again considering succession of bloom, you might consider interplanting Virginia bluebells with some other plant that likes the same conditions so that you won't be stuck with a bare spot for the rest of the growing season. Ferns are a good choice for these conditions. Try cinnamon fern (*Osmunda cinnamomea*) or ostrich fern (*Matteuccia pensylvanica*). The great blue lobelia also is a nice choice.

BACKGROUND

If you have room in the back of the garden for a shrub or two, plant forsythia. Its cheery yellow sprays are a very visible sign of spring. You can cut some branches early and bring them indoors, where they will flower in a vase of water. They'll be the first cut flowers from your garden. In other seasons, forsythia is an attractive green shrub.

A cultivar of spirea called 'Bridal Wreath' also makes a good backdrop. It is a wonderful specimen planting that produces clusters of small white flowers in spring and summer that resemble a bride's bouquet. 'Bridal Wreath' blooms profusely and likes full sun and well-drained soil.

Spirea resembles sprays of tiny bridal bouquets. (Photo by Alan Detrick.)

Both forsythia and 'Bridal Wreath' spirea should be pruned after flowering to maintain vigor and maximum flowering for next year.

OTHER SPRING BLOOMERS

Here are a few other early bulbs that you might consider for your garden.

Winter Aconite

Winter aconite (*Eranthis hyemalis*) is one of the earliest bulbs, blooming in some places in late January and early February. Its yellow blossoms with frilly green collars are often the first sign of spring. They are very hardy, flourish in sun or shade, and will quickly form large colonies. Winter aconite is quite self-sufficient and will never need to be disturbed.

Muscari

Muscari, or grape hyacinth, is a genus of the lily family from the Mediterranean. The spikes of this small bulb are covered with tiny, bell-shaped blue blossoms. This was one of my favorite flowers as a child, and I still love them planted under trees or for underplanting tulips or daffodils. Muscari also comes in white, which looks good with darker-colored companion plantings. The white varieties never seem to look as robust as the blues, though. A double

A river of daffodils leads to an explosion of forsythia. (Photo by Michael Shedlock, New England Stock Photo.)

Muscari (grape hyacinths) are good bedfellows for midseason daffodils.

variety with the ponderous name of *Muscari comosum* 'Plumosum' has always looked to me like a plant-breeding mistake that escaped from the laboratory. Muscari requires no care.

Small Alliums

There are lots of small, early, very pretty alliums that look nice in rock gardens or up front in borders. They come in shades of pink, yellow, and white. Some popular varieties are *Allium moly,* a soft yellow variety; *A. neapolitanum,* which has a white bloom; and *A. flavum,* a deeper yellow allium. There are many other varieties, so consult a bulb catalog for more ideas (see p. 126). McClure & Zimmerman has the most extensive collection I've seen.

Anemones

Another early bloomer is the anemone (*Anemone blanda*). The blooms are useful as a low-growing group or for underplanting daffodils or tulips. The blues are wonderful with yellow daffodils but also great by themselves, as are the pinks and whites. I have seen the whites used as an underplanting for red Kaufmanniana tulips (an 8-in. species), but the result was a bit much.

A small allium brings color to any nook. (Photo by Alan Detrick.)

Corydalis is a great choice for rock gardens. (Photo by Alan Detrick.)

You might have trouble telling the bottom from the top of these small, dark tubers, so look closely. Soak them in water overnight before planting, as they get very dry in storage.

Corydalis

Among this group of low-growing spring flowers, the most popular is the European species *Corydalis bulbosa,* which is native to northern and eastern Europe. Its pink to purple racemes (a raceme is a bunch of pendant blooms on one stem) mix well with other spring flowers because the plant reaches only 6 in. tall. It is great in rock gardens, where it tumbles over walls and steps. It is happy under trees in the spring, when it can get some sun, and doesn't care about summer sun because it goes dormant. You will not find corydalis at your local garden center, but it is common in better catalogs (see p. 126).

Trilliums

The trillium is an American woodland wildflower, a native of cool, moist, acid situations. It is at home in the shade. The easiest of the trillium family for garden culture is *Trillium grandiflorum,* which produces a single flower about 3 in. across with three petals. The flower lasts a long time and will deepen in color from white to light rose. In a drift of trilliums, you will see much color variation. *T. sessile* produces a much smaller, reddish purple flower. This trillium is becoming very rare.

Trilliums are available in catalogs (see p. 126). You will also find these specialty items in the classified sections of garden magazines. Please do not collect them from the wild.

Phlox Subulata

This very short phlox species (3 to 5 in. tall), also known as moss phlox, is widely planted in the United States. That's because it's so easy to grow. It is at home where nothing else wants to grow. It likes sun but is not picky about soil. It is a very good ground cover and will form a dense mat, even in poor soils. It forms a spectacular blanket of pink, white, or purple flowers that happily tumbles over walls, steep banks,

Trillium grandiflorum fits in well in this woodland setting. (Photo by Karen Bussolini.)

Phlox subulata creates a colorful blanket. (Photo by Charles Mann.)

rocks, and any other obstruction, creating a dramatic color display. If you're looking for no-trouble spring color, look no more. *Phlox subulata* pretty much takes care of itself.

Wild Cyclamens

Several varieties of cyclamen are native to North American woodlands. They bloom very early, often pushing up through the snow, and do well under shade trees, where they will form a nice ground cover if they are happy with the situation.

This is not the florist's cyclamen, which is often a large plant with 2-in. blooms and is not winter hardy. This is a small plant with small pink flowers held aloft on individual stems. Wild cyclamens are usually hard to find at a garden store but are readily available through catalogs (see p. 126).

Hardy cyclamen increases from year to year. (Photo by Paddy Wales.)

Pots of spring bulbs make a colorful statement. (Photo by Derek Fell.)

CHAPTER 9

Container Gardening for Spring

YOU REALLY WANT to grow spring bulbs, but you have no piece of ground in which to plant them. No matter. If you have a balcony, a rooftop, or a patio—any sort of outdoor space that gets pretty good sunlight—you can grow many spring bulbs . . . in containers.

THE VESSEL

Many types of containers will work just fine: half a whiskey barrel, a large redwood or cedar planter, an old wash boiler or galvanized iron tub, or a couple of automobile or truck tires stacked one upon the other. Just about anything that will hold the planting medium together will do, as long as it has some drainage holes in the bottom. I do not recommend clay pots, since the freezing and thawing that occurs in winter may break them, or plastic, which tends to get brittle and crack in the cold. If there are no drainage holes in the bottom, drill or punch a number of them. This is very important, as the bulbs will rot without proper drainage.

Place the container on three or four bricks or terra-cotta pot feet (available from garden centers or catalogs such as Gardeners Eden, Lee Valley Tools Ltd., or Smith & Hawken; see p. 129) to make sure there is a channel for water to drain out. This is important, because if the container won't drain, you will soon have

soil soup inside, and all your bulbs will rot. Be sure to elevate the container *before* you fill it. Otherwise, unless you are Charles Atlas, you won't be able to move it later.

THE MEDIUM

Fill the bottom of the container with about 2 in. of gravel or other material approximately the same size to insulate the drainage holes from the potting medium and to make sure they don't get clogged. Another satisfactory material for drainage is a bucket full of those plastic "peanuts" used for shipping.

In a tub or several buckets, mix up a growing medium of three parts potting soil, two parts vermiculite, and one part milled sphagnum moss. This will give you a growing medium that has some organic matter in it and won't get hard and compacted.

THE CONTENTS

For a container the size of half a whiskey barrel, you will need about 4 cu. ft. of growing medium. Fill the container to within 12 in. of the top and tamp down the soil. Sprinkle a couple of handfuls of phosphate fertilizer over the soil and cover with another inch of growing medium. At this depth, you can plant daffodils. If they will be your tallest flowers, arrange them toward the center. You can plant them somewhat closer together than you would in the yard, but keep the bulbs a couple of inches apart. Carefully cover them with the soil mixture, making sure they stay upright.

Continue to fill up the container, planting other bulbs at the proper depths. Don't plant these additional bulbs right on top of the daffodils, but to the outside in clumps. When you reach about an inch below the top, tamp down the soil and add more if you need to. Water the bulbs thoroughly, until you see water draining out the bottom. Don't be alarmed by the amount; it will take more water than you might expect. Then just leave it alone. The container will get plenty of water from the elements.

If you plant this container in October in Zone 6, you'll have flowers in April.

FORCING BULBS INDOORS

The term *forcing* means creating an artificial spring. Cutting branches of forsythia in February, bringing them indoors, and placing them in water causes them to burst into bloom. This is

Half of a barrel is home to an entire garden of bulbs. (Photo by Derek Fell.)

considered forcing. The same thing can be accomplished with bulbs (some work much better than others), but in this case you will need to create an artificial winter, too.

Choosing Bulbs for Forcing

In late summer, order bulbs that you want to force. When they arrive in fall, put them in the back of the refrigerator, keep them dry, and leave them until January. The best daffodils for forcing are paper-whites and other daffodils of the tazetta strain (Division 8 in daffodil classification lingo), which grow well in warmer areas. Get a lot of these and plant them at two-week intervals for a succession of bloom.

Put the paper-whites in a bowl about 2 in. deep. Surround them with gravel and fill with water up to the bottom of the bulbs. Do not let the water cover the bulbs completely, or they will rot. Do not let them dry out either. Place them in an area with low light until they start to grow. Then move them to bright, indirect light. In three to five weeks, you will have white blossoms and an enchanting fragrance.

Dutch hyacinths also respond well to artificial winter and spring. After chilling, you can treat them the same as the daffodils or use a forcing jar. A forcing jar has a mouth as wide as a hyacinth bulb, with a lip to hold the bulb upright. The neck is narrower, widening into a bulbous body. The hyacinth bulb sits on the narrow neck with just the root area exposed below. Fill the jar until the water just touches the root area and keep it at that level. Don't let the bulb proper sit in the water. Soon you will see white roots growing down into the water and the flower spike emerging from the top. Dutch hyacinths have a very sweet fragrance.

The other bulb that forces very well is the crocus. Treat it the same as the daffodils. You

A well-planned container planting of bulbs and pansies. (Photo by Derek Fell.)

can force tulips, too, but they always look leggy and out of place to me. I'd reserve them for the outdoors. Consult a catalog for other bulbs to try (see p. 126).

An alternate method of forcing bulbs is to pot them in the fall and store them in a cool (about 40° F), dry, dark place for the required cold period—about 12 weeks. Keep the soil in the pots just slightly moist. At the end of the cool rest period, you will see shoots 1 to 2 in. high. Then bring the bulbs out into the light when you want them to bloom, and water well.

Cineraria makes the main statement in these raised beds. (Photo by Derek Fell.)

CHAPTER 10

The Second Spring Show: Late April through May

THERE ARE SINGULAR BEAUTIES of each part of the growing season, but for sheer exuberance in my area, late April and May has to be the winner. The enthusiasm with which the bulbs and wildflowers fairly fling themselves into bloom is breathtaking and I am amazed each year at how fast it all happens. The spring bloomers have so little time, but, thank Heaven, there are so many.

LATER BULBS AND THEIR COMPANIONS

By late April, only the long leaves of the early bulbs will be left. Although these need to keep growing to nourish the plants for next spring's flowers, you will want some new flowers to occupy your eyes. The bill is easily filled by some later and larger bulbs.

Small Fritillaria

I like *Fritillaria meleagris*. This subtle and unusual plant has little, checkered, pendant bells in a broad range of colors from purple through white. The plants grow 8 to 10 in. tall and are great looking, particularly in a garden that appears somewhat unstructured, like mine. Other short varieties of fritillaria are nice for a

SUGGESTED PLANTINGS	
TALLEST	Peonies, azaleas
TALLER	Large fritillaria, bearded irises, columbine
MEDIUM HEIGHT	Hybrid tulips, bleeding heart
FAIRLY SHORT	Spanish bluebells, English bluebells, dwarf irises
SHORT	Small fritillaria, species tulips, dog's-tooth violets (fill in with pansies)

change of pace, although they are somewhat more expensive. Among these are *F. michail-ovsky*, purple with a yellow edge; the really expensive *F. pallidiflora*, which has a soft yellow blossom with a hint of green; and the astronomically expensive *F. pontica*, which has green flowers with brown edges held on 18-in. stems. Although these natives to Asia Minor have been naturalized along riverbanks in Europe for centuries, they are not well known in America and will cause some comment among visitors to your garden. Plant them as soon as you get them, as they are somewhat perishable. They like cool, shady locations with good drainage. I recommend using them in a mass or a very loosely structured row four or five deep. A caveat: Be sure your source is a commercial grower, not a wild harvester.

Fritillaria meleagris **is a little charmer that's economical and easy to grow. (Photo by Mick Hales.)**

This traditional cottage garden displays Old World charm. (Photo by Karen Bussolini.)

Species Tulips

Unlike the larger hybrid tulips, species, or wild, tulips will come back year after year. They are available in short and medium varieties and can look like a classic Darwin tulip, a wide-open star, or a water lily; they can even sport spidery blooms. One of my favorites is *Tulipa tarda,* from central Asia. Some horticulturists believe that this may be the archetypal tulip. Its flower opens wide to reveal white petals with a yellow base. Easy to grow in a relatively sunny spot, *T. tarda* will increase to become almost like a ground cover. I also like *T. bakeri* 'Lilac Wonder', which grows just 6 in. tall and has purple petals with a lemon yellow base. You'll love it. You'll also love *T. biflora.* At barely 3 in. tall, it is the world's smallest tulip and a real charmer. There are many others as well. I suggest that you get a catalog from McClure *&* Zimmerman or Van Engelen for a more complete listing (see p. 126). You will not find many (if any) of these at your local garden store.

Dog's-Tooth Violets

If you have a spot that's partially shaded and stays moist most of the time (not dripping wet, just sort of damp), try dog's-tooth violets, or erythronium. They are about 12 in. tall and look just like miniature lilies in purple, pink, yellow, or white. In fact, another name for them is trout lily, because they thrive near streams. Try the cultivar called 'Frans Hals', an imperial purple. Warning: Dog's-tooth violets often take a year to settle in before presenting you with flowers. You may think they died off during the winter, but don't give up on them. They're just gathering strength. This is a woodland flower, so plant it 5 to 6 in. deep in a spot where it will get some shade—under shrubs or around the edge of a larger plant.

Spanish and English Bluebells

Spanish bluebells are a showstopper and a great second-tier planting, growing taller than the small tulips and dog's-tooth violets. Another member of the lily family, they are a form of scilla and are also called squill. More people stop to ask me about my bluebells than about any other flower in the garden. The plants come back year after year, stronger than ever, and require almost nothing but a little sun each day. I have some in the open and some under a birch tree, and they do equally well in both spots. They come in blue, pink, and white. I prefer blue, but the pink are quite attractive, too. They are best planted in a clump, 6 to 8 in. deep, where they can accent a corner. Their leaves will shrivel and disappear in June, at which time you can add some shallow-rooted plant on top.

English bluebells are violet and not as robust in appearance as Spanish bluebells. However, appearances can be deceiving. The delicate-looking flowers increase rapidly, and in open shade can produce the lovely bluebell meadows so beloved in England. They will even interbreed with their Spanish cousins to fill a place they like, which to an English bluebell means dappled shade. This is good if you like bluebells. Lucky for me, I do.

Dwarf Irises

Dwarf irises (*Iris reticulata*), at about 8 in., are also nice for color. They will multiply quickly into drifts so thick that you may have to thin them out after a while. I like to plant them in mixed colors of blue, yellow, white, and bronze. Although a solid color low in the garden as an underplanting for taller bulbs is commendable, these little irises are so interesting and textured that I think mixing them is better. To prevent a new planting from looking too structured, toss a handful in one spot and plant them where they happen to land.

Hybrid Tulips

In this higher tier (14 to 28 in.), hybrid tulips make a great statement, but you need to plant them in a mass. Tall tulips (2 ft. or more) look silly by themselves. Mixed colors are really fine, and I don't know why more gardeners don't use them this way. A solid-color planting, however, attracts attention dramatically and is great if you're doing a one-color garden. Choose your colors carefully so that the tulips don't dominate your garden. If you have two dozen red tulips together, interplant them with something

Iris reticulata is a sea of blue and green. (Photo by Mick Hales.)

else, or you won't see anything except those tulips. But two dozen or more white or blue tulips . . . that's good.

Hybrid tulips will not winter over well for a second year's show. A few may return, but they will be kind of spindly. Even so, these tulips are worth it . . . maybe about 100 each year. If you are going to buy large quantities, check out the Van Engelen catalog (see p. 128).

Plant tulips 6 in. deep and give them a top-dressing of phosphate in the fall and early spring. Don't worry about additional fertilizer, as I consider these tulips to be expendable.

Pansies

Where you have gaps in your garden, fill in with pansies. Pansies are inexpensive to buy by the flat and are a simple way to bring color to bare spots. They are available in almost any color to match the scheme you have in mind.

'Crystal Bowl' pansies are the front men for 'Golden Oxford' tulips. (Photo by Alan Detrick.)

Also try their more understated cousin, the viola. Violas are smaller but very charming, and with some care, they will come back for years. A small species known as Johnny-jump-up accomplishes a return very handily. A variety called 'Arkwright's Ruby', which is a stunning red, is available at a high price by mail from several catalogs, including Wayside. Go to your local garden center instead.

TALL-GROWING BULBS AND COLUMBINE

Next in the progression are the tall fritillaria, irises, and columbine.

Fritillaria Persica

Fritillaria persica has tall spires with plum-colored bells. It grows more than 3 ft. tall, so it may need staking. This subtle plant reminds me of a Cambodian temple, with progressively narrowing dark spires like those at Angkor Wat. The flowers are dusky, as is the gray-green foliage. It is not common in American gardens and will lend an air of somberness and reserve to your garden as its dark spires rise above the emerging summer foliage. The gardener who grows *F. persica* is obviously wise and mysterious, a master of understatement.

The large bulbs of this fritillaria like to be planted about 8 in. deep in partial sun. They also like a top-dressing of phosphate fertilizer in spring when the leaves appear.

Fritillaria Imperialis

If *F. persica* is understated and somber, *F. imperialis* is anything but. It is the sitting monarch of the spring bulb world, the biggest lion in the pride. *F. imperialis* does, in fact, seem to wear a crown. Atop a stalk that can reach 3 ft. tall appears a rosette of 8 to 10 pendant flowers topped by a tuft of attractive green foliage. The flowers can be orange, red, or yellow. All are spectacular, the yellow being the least showy (but perhaps the most tasteful) of the bunch. You would expect to see a forest nymph wearing this crown.

If you have a problem with plant poachers, you will not want this plant. Unfortunately, it is a very strong "harvester" magnet. But if your garden is secure, it will be a highlight of your spring show.

Irises

The bearded, or German, iris is the most familiar of the genus in the United States. It is very showy and comes in virtually any color.

Irises are best planted in the late summer or early fall and should be clumped together—one iris by itself looks like Wilt Chamberlain visiting Munchkin Land. You will not be able to over-plant them with anything else because they are shallow rooters and the long, swordlike leaves need to grow all summer to make enough food for next year's blooms, so pick a spot where this won't bother you. The flowers are so wonderful, though, that they're worth the short blooming period. You can interplant them with spring- and fall-blooming crocuses to good effect.

Irises need plenty of sun. They don't need it all day, but if they don't get about six hours' worth, they won't bloom well. Plant the rhizomes (the thickened underground portion of the stem that stores food) 1 in. deep, just barely under the soil, and 12 in. apart.

You would do well to pick the more subdued colors of the bearded iris. There are lots of nice

A fearless New York City gardener stakes his claim on East 20th Street.

Japanese irises look like large butterflies. (Photo by Charles Mann.)

blues (even running to black in the variety called 'Superstition'), deep reds, light pinks, and soft yellows. Avoid anything that calls so much attention to itself that your garden audience will see nothing else. These would include the oranges, hot pinks, and what are referred to as the "startling bicolors." There is a green variety that should be named "Ghastly." The dignity of the stately darker colors and subdued pastels attracts quite enough attention without resorting to the type of overstatement provided by it.

If your garden has lots of sun and damp ground, try the Japanese iris. These irises have flatter and somewhat larger flowers than German irises. They are available in many wonderful colors and resemble a group of large butterflies hovering over your garden. They bloom in early summer.

The English iris blooms in June and is a bulbous, rather than a tuberous (or rhizomatous, if you want to get technical), plant. It has spiky leaves and produces blooms in various shades of blue with a golden splash on the blade. The English iris is not bearded like the German iris and is easy to grow, given enough sun.

The Dutch iris also blooms in early summer. It is about 16 in. tall and comes in a variety of colors with blossoms reminiscent of orchids. It is hardy, easy to grow, and cheap! At a dime apiece or less, the Dutch iris is one of the best bargains in the bulb world.

If you like irises, you also should look into the Spanish iris, Louisiana iris, and Siberian iris, as well as other, rarer types. All are rewarding.

Columbine

Columbine is one of my all-time favorites. It is native to the northern states and Canada, common in the dappled shade of eastern fencerows. One wild form, *Aquilegia canadensis,* is red and yellow with short spurs, but it has now been bred to produce many wonderful colors with long spurs. There are also short varieties with no spurs, which are attractive for the front of a border. The taller varieties grow 2 to 3 ft. tall and are prolific bloomers, producing an airy cloud of outrageously beautiful flowers that, from a distance, have no apparent support. This is because the stems are very thin and wiry.

Columbine thrives in a partially shaded garden, where it will interbreed with its fellows, producing new colors every year. Bloom begins in May and often continues to the end of July or even into August. You will get lots of favorable comments about your columbine.

Columbine is not difficult to start from seed, and if you're going to use a lot of plants, it might be worth the effort. It is usually sold as a large plant at garden centers and green markets, so it can be expensive.

Aquilegia canadensis **is the native American form of columbine. (Photo by Mick Hales.)**

Do not put winter mulch over the crown of the plant, as this may inhibit its regrowth in spring. Though perennial, columbine is not long-lived. But it is such a prolific self-seeder that you will probably never run out of it.

THE BACKDROP

For the tall species for your garden, consider peonies, azaleas, and rhododendrons.

Peonies

Peonies are not shrubs, but herbaceous plants, meaning they do not have woody stems. Their foliage dies back to underground root stocks after frost and reappears in the spring. Peonies are very hardy and have spectacular blossoms. They have high resistance to pests and blithely endure cold that would paralyze a penguin. They need lots of sun; six hours a day is the minimum, but more is better.

Peonies do not like wet feet, so plant them where there's good drainage. The saucer-size blossoms come in both double and single forms. These days, the doubles seem to be more common. In fact, when my singles bloom, people ask if they are some type of rose. I like the singles better. They open with wanton abandon, sort of flinging themselves at the world. The doubles are like ladies with lots of petticoats, much more demure.

Don't worry about the ants that swarm all over peony buds. They are not eating the flower but a nectar it exudes. Folk wisdom has it that the ants and the peonies have a symbiotic relationship: The ants eat the outer covering off the bud, allowing the flower to open. This is *not* correct.

Fall is the best time to plant peonies. Dig a deep hole with your spade and slip the plant from its container, disturbing the roots as little as possible. Peonies need lots of nourishment and will appreciate some fertilizer that is high in phosphorus (the middle number in the formula) mixed in with the soil. Apply some of this fertilizer in early spring around the plant but away from the crown. Set the plant so that

Peonies complement a small Japanese maple. (Photo by Paddy Wales.)

the shoots are 1 to 2 in. beneath the soil, then water them well. Peonies will not bloom if they're planted too deep.

Peony blossoms are heavy, so the plant may need staking. The best way to do this is to place four thin bamboo stakes at the compass points of the plant. Be careful not to drive them into the roots. There are also wire stakes with loops that are very good for this. Lee Valley Tools Ltd., Smith & Hawken, and Gardeners Eden carry these (see p. 129). Tie a string or a long twist tie from stake to stake to surround the plant completely. This will keep the stems from falling over without inhibiting growth.

Very rarely, peonies fall victim to a fungal disease called botrytis. The leaves and buds become shriveled and black. This probably won't happen to your plant, but if it does, cut all the foliage down and destroy it. Apply a fungicide, such as benomyl, to what's left and wait for next year.

Azaleas

Azaleas, a part of the rhododendron family, are the mainstay of spring in the South. Stop by Bryan Park in Richmond, Virginia, on an April afternoon. It is the azalea capital of the world and one of the most captivating sights I have ever seen. Azaleas are the staple there, not the background. However, they'll make a great background for your garden . . . *if* they have acid soil. They are very picky about that. If your soil tests alkaline or even neutral, add something to decrease the pH. Aluminum sulfate is good. A commercial preparation that contains a fertilizer, such as Miracid, also works well.

I like the pink and lavender shades of azaleas, but they also come in red, white, apricot, and yellow. Just don't fall for the fluorescent reds; they don't go with anything.

Azaleas like good drainage and do well in shady situations, such as the dappled shade of an open wood. They are very tolerant of low temperature, surviving winters of –20°F and

A pink rhododendron and a white azalea happily share space in New York's Gramercy Park.

summers of over 100°F. Some are evergreen but most are deciduous, meaning they lose their leaves in winter.

Spring is the best time to plant azaleas. This gives them time to get established before their first winter. Evergreen azaleas lose a good deal of water through their leaves in winter, and this can kill a newly planted specimen. Azaleas are shallow rooters, so don't plant them too deep—no more than 1 in. of soil over the rootball—and about 3 ft. apart to allow growing room. Do not prune them unless they take on an unpleasing shape. Check the soil for acidity each spring.

Rhododendron

Rhododendrons are woody shrubs with long, oval, evergreen leaves. Some varieties grow up to 10 ft. tall. They come in an astounding variety of colors, even blue in a superior variety called 'Blue Peter'. The flowers are carried in clusters at the ends of the branches.

Rhododendrons are easy to grow, given the right conditions. The right conditions are the same as those for azaleas and other woodland denizens: light, well-drained soil that is high in humus, partial shade, and soil acidity. They enjoy a summer mulch to retain moisture and keep weeds down. It is not a good idea to perform heavy-duty weeding around a rhododendron, as many roots are near the surface.

OTHER GREAT PERFORMERS

Of course, there are hundreds, even thousands, of other plants you could try out in your garden. If you are new to gardening and don't want any disappointments, let me recommend a few that are beloved by gardeners. (If you hear a plant is beloved by gardeners, this means it will grow, reliably, almost anywhere it can reasonably be expected to do so. Otherwise, it would *not* be beloved by gardeners!)

Bleeding Heart

Dicentra spectabilis is the old-fashioned bleeding heart grown in millions of American gardens. I have always loved this plant. It grew in our rock garden when I was a child, and it is probably my second oldest flower memory (violets are the first). It is native to the woodlands of Japan and Asia. It has deep rose, heart-shaped flowers that hang one after another from fairly long branches, so you often get 12 or more in a row. It blooms in May in a partially shaded location, and the flowers persist well into June. A white variety is nice for a change.

These plants can grow nearly 3 ft. tall, so space them far apart. They also are moderately good self-seeders, and you will find little plants around the base of the parent. You can recognize them by their distinctive leaf shape. *D. spectabilis* is easy to grow and tolerant of most conditions. When the foliage turns yellow in the middle of summer, you can cut it down. The plant will last for many years.

D. x 'Luxuriant' is so different from *D. spectabilis* as to be almost unrecognizable. The blossoms appear in sprays from upright stalks above low, ferny foliage and are much smaller than those of *D. spectabilis*. The plants are very hardy and spread at an uncanny rate by self-seeding. They are valuable as a fill-in for any spot in the garden and will act on their own. If

Old-fashioned bleeding heart and Spanish blue-bells seem to enjoy each other's company. (Photo by Paddy Wales.)

you don't want them, just pull them up. They're easy to identify by their deeply cut, ferny foliage. They will reward you for uprooting them by coming up someplace else.

Geraniums

These are the *true* geraniums (*Geranium* spp.), not the pelargoniums that most Americans call geraniums. True geraniums are single-flowered (although there are plenty of blossoms) and generally low growing. They like sun but will tolerate some shade. They come in blues and pinks, and the shorter varieties make a nice ground cover. Different species of geraniums bloom in succession from early spring throughout most of the summer.

Heuchera

Also known as coral bells, *Heuchera sanguinea* has gained an enormous following in the past 20 years, and deservedly so. It is native to the mountains of western North America, so it knows what Americans like: lots of flowers and no trouble. Heuchera fills the bill. It produces sprays of light pink to red flowers from May into August, sometimes on stems so long that they need a thin bamboo stake to hold them up. At other times, heuchera is a low mound of attractive green, sometimes mottled, foliage. The round leaves stay green through most of the winter in Zone 6. Heuchera will grow in almost any conditions, but it prefers well-drained, humus-rich soil. Do not put winter mulch over the crown of the plant.

Heuchera, also known as coral bells, produces flowers that rise above the leaves on almost invisible stems. (Photo by Charles Mann.)

FOR THE SHADY GARDEN

Many first-time gardeners dismiss a shady patch of ground as unworkable for a garden spot. Nothing could be further from the truth. There are many plants that thrive in shade, including hosta and astilbe (both virtually indestructible), which are discussed in Chapter 13.

Ferns, caladiums, elephant's ear, and begonias are among the other plants you may want to consider for your shady areas.

Ferns

In the total shade of a low spot in the woods or in dappled shade, you may notice the shoots of young fern growth. These are called fiddleheads because they look just like the top of a bass viol or a cello. Ferns are great plants for a shady garden. The taller varieties, such as the ostrich fern, provide a nice green backdrop.

Ferns are very old, useful plants. They have successfully competed for their livelihood since before there were trees, before flowers, and certainly much before grasses. In fact, some ferns have been around for 350 million years! When the first amphibians slithered ashore from the sea, the ferns greeted them.

Despite their age, this ancient line of plants has lost none of its vigor. There are some 12,000 species of ferns in the world today, 250 of them native Americans.

Ferns prosper in shade—under trees, in the shadows of buildings, and in other places where few things grow. Some varieties will form a tall ground cover in full sun. They are very prolific

Fiddleheads unroll with eerie speed. (Photo by Mick Hales.)

Ferns make great pot plants for shade. (Photo by Derek Fell.)

and spread rapidly by underground runner in moist conditions. Ferns also will spread by spore, but this process requires more stringent conditions to be met. They are great for filling in shady spots, and the many shapes, textures, and colors (some have bronze- or silver-tinted fronds) make this an interesting proposition.

Caladiums

Caladiums are tender, tuberous-rooted plants that add great color to a very shady spot. They cannot be planted outdoors until all danger of frost has passed, but after that, put them in a shady corner and watch it fill with color.

Caladiums have large, up-facing, heart-shaped leaves in a whole spectrum of whites, pinks, and reds. They like damp, rich soil and do not tolerate sun at all. I use them under a birch tree as a backdrop for impatiens.

You can buy small caladiums in pots from a garden store or green market, or you can start them yourself from the tubers in late winter. Put each tuber in a small pot filled with potting mix. Cover very lightly with more mix. Water thoroughly but do not soak, as this will cause the tubers to rot. Place the pot in bright, indirect light and keep the soil damp, not soggy. Be patient. Caladiums will form roots before they put forth shoots.

Elephant's Ear

Elephant's ear (*Colocasia esculenta*) is aptly named, for these big, green, caladium-like plants often produce leaves more than 2 ft. long. In the tropics, they produce a huge, succulent fruit (hence *esculenta*). In your garden, they'll grow stems as tall as 3 to 5 ft. They make an excellent background plant and thrive in dense shade.

This plant will grow in any sort of soil with good drainage. You can dig the bulbs in fall, dry them off, and winter them over to replant in spring. The bulbs will increase in size from year to year and will produce offshoots, which you can replant. Soon you'll have a dozen elephant's ears instead of one.

Caladiums bring color to the deepest shade. (Photo by Mick Hales.)

Begonias

There are more kinds of begonias than you can count, but they generally fall into three categories: fibrous, tuberous, and rhizomatous.

The fibrous begonias will tolerate sun where it doesn't get too hot (over 90°F). They are mostly used for bedding plants.

For the shady garden, you will want to concern yourself with the tuberous varieties, which produce lovely rose- or camellia-shaped blossoms up to 3 in. across in almost any color except blue. You can grow them from their tiny, dustlike seeds (the hard way), or you can buy the tubers (the easy way). After all danger of frost has passed, plant the tubers 10 or 12 in. apart in a shady location. The top of the tuber has a slight depression that should face up. Do not completely cover the tuber, just surround it with soil. Water well but don't allow water to

Begonias form the key color element in this shady arrangement. (Photo by Derek Fell.)

stand in the depression, or the tuber will rot. Shoots will soon appear from the depression. You can also start tuberous begonias in pots indoors to get a jump on the season.

Rhizomatous begonias, also known as Rex begonias, are grown primarily for their richly mottled foliage in shades of purple, white, silver, and green. The taller varieties make a colorful background in a warm but shady spot. Rhizomatous begonias do have small flowers, but their main attraction is their colorful leaves.

If you want to know more about begonias, there are lots of books on the subject. Growing begonias is a very specialized field, with begonia societies and begonia clubs. If you want to try begonias, be prepared for some disappointments. For instance, tuberous begonias are somewhat fussy about moisture and will rot away with astonishing speed if they're too wet.

SUMMER VACATION FOR HOUSEPLANTS

After any danger of frost has passed, consider taking your houseplants out to the garden for the summer. Many of them perk up considerably. There are, however, exceptions. For instance, there is no point in taking an African violet outside. The sun will burn its leaves, and rain will spot them. I don't take jade plants out anymore either. They would get so waterlogged from rain that they would fall over. Most other plants appreciate the outdoors.

When you take a plant outdoors, it will need to go through the process of *hardening off*. This is acclimating the plant to the conditions of its new environment, light, and temperature. Some people advise taking a plant out for an hour one day, two hours the next, and so on until it can be out for the whole day. This is fine, but I don't have time to be schlepping plants in and out, and I'll bet you don't either.

Here's a better solution: Take the plants outdoors and put them in shade for a couple of days. Then move them to light shade. After a couple more days, move the sun lovers to a spot where they'll get morning sun and shade in the afternoon. Finally, move them to full sun, depending on their individual needs. Remember to water plants in full sun frequently; shade lovers require less frequent watering. Since they're not in garden soil, the plants will still need to be on their regular feeding schedule.

Summer vacation can greatly revitalize clivia, as is evident from this plant, recently brought indoors. (Photo by Erik Simmons.)

Here is a great arrangement of colors and shapes for a patio or deck. (Photo by Derek Fell.)

CHAPTER 11
Container Gardening for Summer

PLANTS IN CONTAINERS do wonders to cheer up a balcony, patio, or deck. Please do not confine yourself to the ubiquitous geraniums (properly, pelargoniums) or petunias. Many much more interesting plants can be grown very successfully in pots and tubs. The following are a few examples.

LILIES

Lilies are among the easiest plants to grow in containers outdoors, and they are extremely rewarding, as the flowers are quite large, colorful, and usually fragrant. Any kind of lily you want to try in a pot will most likely succeed. Asian and oriental hybrids are good choices because they don't grow too tall and will probably not need staking.

A 10- or 12-in. pot will be big enough for these lilies. Make sure you provide good drainage with gravel or some other material in the bottom of the pot. Lilies are really very durable, but they will not survive standing in water.

If you start several strains at once, you can create a continuous series of bloom. Plant the bulbs 6 to 8 in. deep in a good potting mix (such as the mix described in Chapter 6) and remember to water them frequently. A large plant like the lily can transpire a surprising amount of water in one day. When the period of bloom is over, let the foliage mature until fall. If you cut a lily blossom for indoors, be sure to leave at least two-thirds of the stalk so that the bulb will have the resources to manufacture enough food to store for the winter. In the fall, move the pots to a sheltered location and bring them out again in the spring.

Potted lilies are the stars of a patio. (Photo by Derek Fell.)

AGAPANTHUS

Agapanthus africanus, or lily-of-the-Nile, is an ideal plant for a patio or deck because it is large and showy, and the bloom—clusters of blue or white flowers on 36-in. stems—lasts for two months. This lily grows from a tuber, and its culture is very easy, requiring only full sun or light shade and a rich soil with good drainage. This South African native will do fine outdoors all year in Southern California or Florida, but north of Zone 9, you will need to bring it indoors for the winter.

TUBEROUS BEGONIAS

Tuberous begonias do very nicely in pots as long as they don't get much sun. A little morning sun won't hurt, but hot afternoon sun will quickly burn their leaves. Some grow upright to almost 2 ft. Others are prostrate and are meant for hanging baskets.

These begonias can produce large flowers—some shaped like camellias, some like roses—often with an edge of a complementary color. By removing the side, or lateral, buds behind the main, or terminal, bud, you will encourage plant growth.

PERENNIALS ON THE PATIO

Many of our familiar garden perennial plants can be grown successfully in containers. I recommend you try some of the hardiest to get started. Be sure to use a large, weatherproof container that will withstand freezes, and make lots of drainage holes in the bottom so the plant won't drown.

In addition to the hardy examples given here, there are many other garden plants that will thrive in containers, and I urge you to experiment. (If a plant grows in the garden where you live, it will probably do well on your terrace.) Just make sure the growing conditions and the

Nicotiana and 'Freckle Face' belamcanda frame the view from a city terrace. (Photo by Karen Bussolini.)

weather conditions are right. And remember that *any* potted plant will need your care more than a plant growing in its natural habitat.

Peonies

Peonies are among the most reliable of plants. You have to try hard to kill a peony. I have seen a neighbor's potted peony in glorious bloom after the hardest of winters.

Plant your peony in regular garden soil, but not too deeply. The crown should be only an inch deep or it will not bloom. Feed the plant with a water-soluble fertilizer, one that you would use with houseplants. Do not use manure. Keep the plant well watered, but not soggy. Some mulch is beneficial to help retain moisture. Peonies need six or seven hours of sun a day, so keep that in mind as you choose a site for your container.

Columbine

I can remember being very surprised to see wild columbine, *A. canadensis,* growing on a rooftop, but it is a champion performer and very easy to grow. In fact, you can sow the seeds directly into the container. As long as you provide enough water, columbine really needs no other care. And you will have bloom every spring, as it self-seeds very well.

Roses

Roses make very good container plants. Any kind of rose will do. Even the fussy hybrid tea roses do fine, perhaps because they aren't exposed to soil-borne diseases and fungi that go after them in the garden. English roses are an excellent choice, because their blooming period is very long-lasting.

Roses will appreciate feeding in the spring and again in June. A water-soluble rose food, like Miracle-Gro for roses, is a good choice, but do not feed roses later than August. Late feeding will cause a new spurt of green growth right when they ought to be going dormant for the winter. In late fall wrap the plants in burlap to protect them from the winter winds and ice.

Pine cones on the 50th Floor? Why not? (Photo by Karen Bussolini.)

Trees

Trees make delightful terrace plantings and do not require as much care as other plantings. Small pines, such as the mugo pine, are an excellent choice. A slow-growing cultivar of blue spruce, such as 'Montgomery', also makes a spectacular specimen plant. The better plant catalogs (see p. 126) or your local nursery will tell you which trees are slow growers.

But a potted tree will need more care than one growing in the ground. Trees require good drainage, so choose a large container and make lots of holes in the bottom. When you plant your tree, plant it only as deep as it is in the pot you bought it in. Otherwise, the trunk will rot. Feed it with a mild water-soluble plant food in the spring (fish emulsion works well). Do not feed your tree in the fall because this will cause new green growth, which will be killed by freezing temperatures.

CHAPTER 12

Early Summer: June through Mid-July

THERE IS A TRICK to keeping your pansies, columbine, and other summer flowers in bloom for a long time: You must cut off the old flower heads before they form seeds, a practice known as *deadheading.* The plant's main mission, of course, is to perpetuate the species, not to make you sigh over the flowers. So, when you remove its potential progeny by removing the faded flowers, it just keeps right on trying to reproduce by making more flowers. (Sooner or later, of course, you will overlook a seed pod and the columbine will have won its victory over your management technique, but deadheading really does prolong bloom.) This is a good technique to keep many flowering plants in bloom. It also keeps the garden looking tidy.

Deadheading will not prolong the blooms of bulbous plants because the finite number of blossoms the bulb will produce are already present in the bulb. Once they're gone, that's it until next year. What it *will* do for bulbous plants is prevent them from wasting energy by trying to produce seeds and concentrate that energy on beefing up the bulb for next year.

THE SUMMER SHOW BEGINS

White pansies with dark faces and cool lavender impatiens make great lower-level plantings. Pansies and the shorter varieties of impatiens are great for filling in the gaps where bulbs were blooming earlier in the year. They are rather shallow-rooted, so they won't bother the deeper-planted bulbs, and they will fit in with any color scheme.

A note about impatiens: This has become a very popular plant—trite, even, to some garden writers. However, impatiens is one of the most reliable, useful plants in the garden. It can be depended upon to bring brightness and color to almost any spot that needs it. It is predictable and well mannered; it stays where you put it and doesn't create successive generations that you can't get rid of. You can't go wrong with impatiens, ever.

SUGGESTED PLANTINGS

TALLEST	Tall alliums, daylilies
TALLER	White or pink foxgloves, ladybells, goatsbeard
MEDIUM HEIGHT	Blue Canterbury bells, Asiatic lilies, tiger lilies
FAIRLY SHORT	Columbine (mixed shades), small species lilies
SHORT	White pansies, lavender impatiens

THE GARDEN IN EARLY SUMMER

A Azalea

B Ferns

C Columbine

D *Helleborus orientalis*

E Evening primrose

F Hydrangea

G Hosta

H Lilies

I Jack-in-the-pulpit

J Birch tree

K Impatiens

L Rhododendron

M Daylilies

N Early monkshood

O *Fritillaria persica*

P 'Stella de Oro' daylilies

Q *Fritillaria meleagris*

R Climbing rose

S Foxglove

T Boxwood

U Ladybells

V Peony

W Bearded iris

X Canterbury bells

Y Veronica

Z Lady's-mantle

AA Species lilies

BB Crab apple

CC Spiderwort

DD Tall allium

EE Ivy

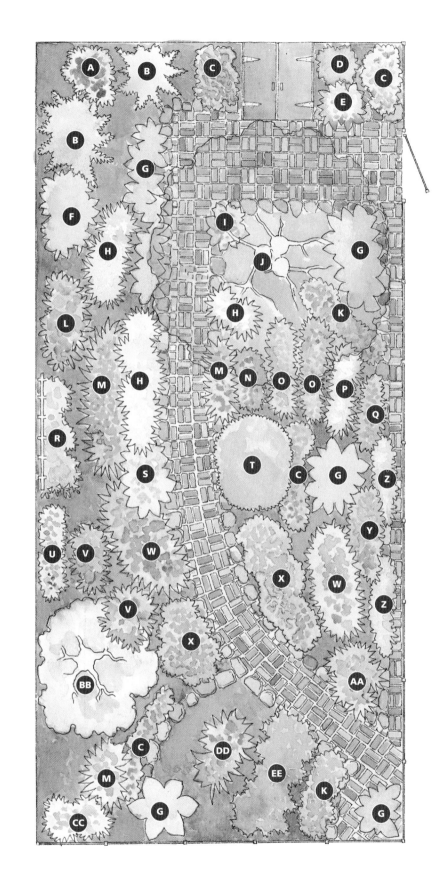

The archetypal cottage garden featuring foxgloves. (Photo by Mick Hales.)

Potted impatiens bring color to ubiquitous pachysandra. (Photo by Karen Bussolini.)

At the next level, the tireless columbine keeps right on blooming. Columbine is an excellent choice to provide eye-catching color at a mid-range height (about 30 in.). Two very good performers are the McKana Giant Hybrids strain and the Spring Song strain. Both have a wide range of colors. These are common offerings in many catalogs. Columbine self-seeds very well and you will have a number of interesting colors resulting from cross-pollination.

SUMMER STAPLES

Your garden has been warming up all spring for the beginning of this season of maximum bloom. It's a time in my garden for the majority of the blues and pinks and whites—a little cooler than the later days of summer when the yellow of black-eyed Susans dominates. The season begins delicately, but leads to a resounding crescendo.

Species Lilies
Small species, or wild, lilies are a charming accent. They don't grow much taller than 12 to 14 in., and they have small flowers that are shaped exactly like the big Turk's-cap lilies. A species known as *Lilium pumilum* is great fun

to look at, with its eye-catching red blossoms. People will say, "That little thing looks just like a lily."

Species lily bulbs are small and white, about the size of a Brazil nut. As with all lilies, plant them where they won't be disturbed by any other planting you may do. One cautionary note: The young plants look remarkably like weeds. If you're not sure about it, leave it alone till it blooms. Give the youngster a chance to grow up before you decide it's a felon.

Butterfly Lilies

A strain of lilies known as Butterfly Lilies, bred by Columbia-Platte Lilies in Oregon, is a great source of color this time of year. I use them to fill in where there were daffodils earlier and where there will be self-seeding cleome later. They are charming and are available in many colors. They look great planted among lower-growing flowers or mixed with columbine or Canterbury bells.

Brodiaea

'Queen Fabiola' brodiaea produces umbels of lovely violet blossoms on 24-in. stems, a little surprising for such a small bulb. Another nice feature of brodiaea is that the plants are cheap, around a dime apiece from Van Engelen and not much more from John Scheepers (see p. 128).

Plant brodiaea in a sunny spot about 3 in. deep. Like most bulbs, it prefers good drainage. It blooms in June.

Canterbury Bells

Columbine, with its long, airy stems, forms a semitransparent layer that is backed up nicely by a denser layer of delicate blue campanulas, or Canterbury bells. *Campanula* has the same root as *campanile,* an Italian word meaning bell tower, and these flowers do look like little bell towers. Canterbury bells vary from 8 in. to 6 ft. tall. In my garden, the taller ones are very useful at their position about halfway back. They begin to bloom in June and continue into July. Canterbury bells self-seed beautifully, so all you need to do is leave them standing until the seedpods have opened. You will find some growing where you don't want them next year. Use your editorial eye and pull up the ones you don't want.

Asiatic Lilies

Asiatic lilies go nicely with Canterbury bells, which provide a lavender-blue backdrop for the lilies. Asiatic lilies are generally shorter than

Canterbury bells serve as a willing anchor for the early summer garden. (Photo by Charles Mann.)

the wild, woodland variety, mostly under 3 ft. The blossoms are up-facing, and they come in a variety of wonderful colors, all of which seem to mix with the Canterbury bells just fine. They will make your garden look very sophisticated. You can leave these lilies undisturbed, and they will continue to present you with blooms for years.

Lilies like to be planted about 8 in. deep in humus-rich, well-drained soil. The root end is obvious in most lily bulbs. Plant it down, with the scales facing up. Asiatic and oriental lilies can be grown in full sun or partial shade.

Asiatic lilies also can be grown quite successfully in pots. They will add sophistication to your patio or deck or even to a sunny window. In the window, you'll have to remember to turn them every couple of days, as they are heliotropic and will try to follow the sun, which results in a very lopsided lily.

It's best to grow the shorter lily varieties in pots, as the taller lilies often need staking. Plant the lily bulb about 6 in. deep, with the roots down, in a potting mixture of soil, vermiculite, and sphagnum moss.

Tiger Lilies
Lilium lancifolium, previously called *L. tigrinum,* is an old and honored member of the June garden. It has been cultivated for thousands of years. Originally only orange with prominent black "freckles," it has been bred into white, yellow, pink, and red varieties as well. I have always been partial to the orange, which is a real show-off, but it's nice to know tiger lilies can now fit in with a more subdued garden scheme, too. They love acid soils and despise alkaline soils, where they will not succeed, so site them accordingly.

Tiger lilies reproduce very successfully by forming little bulblets at the base of the leaves. These fall off and can produce a dense colony within a few years.

Foxgloves
A little deeper in the garden comes an echo in the form of another bell tower shape, the foxgloves. Foxgloves provide some visual interest with the sharp vertical lines of their spires. Individually, the blossoms look like little gloves for foxes, although the name is actually a corruption of "folks' gloves," meaning the "little folks" of Celtic legend. Their colors usually range from pink or purple to light yellow, but I recently saw a white variety, *Digitalis purpurea* 'Gloxinaflora', that is simply stunning. I am plotting where I can put it in my limited space.

The foxglove has been a staple in English gardens for hundreds of years and is the source of the drug digitalis, used for more than 250 years to treat heart problems. *Digitalis* is also the botanical name (genus) of the plant and means "the finger of a glove" in Latin. It is a

Despite their insistent orange, tiger lilies blend well with many colors. (Photo by Derek Fell.)

biennial, one of the tribe that reproduce from seed but usually don't bloom until their second year. This makes getting them started in your garden sort of disconcerting: One year you have them, and the next you don't. This rather vexing situation can be remedied by planting them in two successive years so that you always have another generation on the way. Once they are established, they will flower, set seed, and germinate all in the same year, so they will produce flowers the next. Foxgloves are not reliably hardy as far north as New York City, though. Some years they simply disappear, so be prepared to replant.

There are several varieties, including *D. ambigua* and *D.* x *mertonensis,* that are true perennials. *D. ambigua* is yellow, and *D.* x *mertonensis* is a strawberry color. They do not seem to me to have the vigor of the biennials.

Foxgloves are pretty well behaved. The seeds tend to fall right at the base of the parent, so they won't take over your entire garden.

TALL GROWERS

Although the occasional medium-sized lily or lupine looks very nice in the front of the garden, giving some relief to the eye by breaking up lower planes, the majority of the taller plants belong toward the back. If you have a two-sided garden like mine, the back is toward the wall. If you have a walk-through, you'll site many of the taller plants at the back of the border. But don't make that a firm rule; the element of surprise is one of the greatest in your bag of gardener's tricks.

Daylilies

The daylily, or *Hemerocallis* (meaning "beautiful for one day" and another instance of Greek sneaking into Botanical Latin), is a great plant. It comes in colors ranging from yellow to red, with lots of wonderful shades in between. One of my favorites is 'Prairie Blue Eyes', lavender-blue with a clear yellow throat, but I think the wild orange ones are very pretty, too. Daylilies grow as tall as 3 ft., so they are just right for back-

Short daylilies lead a well-designed progression of summer-blooming flowers. (Photo by Charles Mann.)

ground, although some of the smaller varieties, such as 'Stella de Oro', look very good as accent plants toward the front. Although daylilies are best in the back of my garden, they may look better someplace else in your garden scheme, so use your own judgment. You can always move them later if you change your mind.

The daylily's flower lasts for only one day. That's okay because the tetraploid (genetically manipulated hybrids) plants produce 15 to 30 flowers per stem and hundreds of flowers per

Allium giganteum **puts on a spectacular show. (Photo by Karen Bussolini.)**

plant over the course of a season. It's still a good idea to deadhead them, though. You don't want that plant to devote its attention to seed-making; you want it to make flowers! It's better for cosmetic considerations, too.

Daylilies don't have many serious pests, except aphids. The aphids seem to be at their worst during very hot, dry summers, when they will literally suck the plant dry. Look for aphids near the base of the long leaves. If you find them, a good shot of malathion will save the day. Or you may want to invest in some lady-bugs, whose larvae are the aphid's voracious nemesis. I try not to use pesticides much, but in an emergency situation, I am not above ordering a surgical strike by the air force.

Daylily flowers are edible and make a dramatic addition to a salad (assuming you haven't recently dropped the malathion bomb).

Tall Alliums

The allium is an ornamental bulb that is closely related to the onion and the lily. Do you remember how chives look in flower? It's the same look with allium, only more so. The giant ones, *Allium giganteum,* are 5-in. balls of purple flowers clustered densely on stems that can reach 48 in. tall. They are spectacular and make for a lot of visual interest. I don't grow them because I'm afraid of all that visual interest. I have this recurring nightmare of hordes of flower-hungry "harvesters" ripping them up and selling them on street corners. (If you are a city gardener, you will soon recognize garden para-noia as a self-protective device.)

Instead, I grow *A. christophii,* also known as stars-of-Persia. The more sedate *A. christophii* blooms in late May and early June in Zone 6, and the flowers may last well into July. Its flower heads are less dense than those of *A. giganteum,* looking like a big ball of rather loose-ly packed lilac-colored stars. It grows only about 2 ft. or so tall and is a great choice for planting with daffodils or hostas. When the daffodils are exhausted, stars-of-Persia will attract attention away from the yellowing leaves. With hostas, alliums provide visual interest before the late-summer hosta flowers. Alternatively, you can plant several alliums here and there in the gar-den at random just to break things up (you don't want to be too predictable). You will congratu-late yourself for choosing such a great plant.

Ladybells

Ladybells (*Adenophora*) resemble a little bell tower, looking like a rather leggy version of Canterbury bells, and indeed they are distantly related. The flowers are narrower and the stalks taller than those of Canterbury bells. Ladybells bloom in July and August in lavender-blue, a color not common at that time of year. The plants may need staking during flowering.

Goatsbeard

Goatsbeard (*Aruncus*) is one of those plants you either love or hate. It has sprays of very tiny white flowers carried along branching stems, looking for all the world like an undernourished astilbe. Goatsbeard is very useful as a background plant. Its airy sprays bloom for about three to four weeks in June and then turn brown. The texture of the brown is nice, though, so I let them be. The plant can grow to 5 to 6 ft.

OTHER SUMMER FLOWERS

Many books have been written about all the wonderful flowers of summer. These books are basically lists of everything you could possibly grow. I will not try to duplicate them. Instead, in the following sections, I will tell you about some summer flowers that I have tried with success and that I think you might like.

Lady's-mantle

Alchemilla vulgaris, or lady's-mantle, is a staple in English gardens and does just fine on this side of the Atlantic, too. It is low growing and well behaved. The greenish yellow flowers grow in clusters over leaves that are somewhat hairy and shed water like a mallard. They are good in the front of a border or hanging over a rock wall. Lady's-mantle likes good soil and partial shade but will persevere in the North in full sun. It has no pests and thus is a good choice if you don't want to use pesticides.

Goatsbeard makes an interesting background plant in June.

Lady's-mantle is a hardy and useful fill-in. (Photo by Paddy Wales.)

Clematis is a charming show-off. (Photo by Alan Detrick.)

Clematis

Clematis is a very popular vine with many species, some from North America. Many have been grandly hybridized and are very showy grown on trellises, over fence posts or mailboxes, through climbing roses, and in old trees. The plants are available from catalog houses (see p. 126) and at garden centers. You will find infinitely more variety in the catalogs. Clematis blooms are spectacular and worthwhile in any garden plan with some room; they are a bit grand for really small gardens.

Clematis likes a cool root run and its head in the sun, so plant some low-growing plants around its base to give the root area some shade. Avoid applying a thick coating of mulch, such as shredded bark, because its water-retention abilities will promote rot. Bark chips are fine. Don't be surprised if clematis takes a year or two to become established.

If you have purchased your clematis from a catalog, it will arrive as a mass of long, bare roots. It is advisable to get any bare-root stock in the ground as soon as possible. Soak the roots in lukewarm water for a couple of hours. Dig a

Lupines in a large group can be very imposing. (Photo by Charles Mann.)

Balloonflowers add interest in any situation. (Photo by Janet Loughrey.)

Solomon's-seal is a natural in a church garden. The white flowers have an enchanting fragrance.

hole large enough and deep enough so that you can spread the long roots out away from the crown. Set the crown on a hill of soil in the hole so that the crown is level with your garden soil. Drape the roots down the sides of the hill, fill the hole, and water well. If you don't provide a big enough hole, it will retard the growth of even the healthiest clematis.

Lupines

Lupines are a favorite in English gardens but not so common in America. We think they need England's drippy weather to do well, but they don't. Today's hybrids, developed by the pioneer English plant breeder George Russell, come in many lovely bicolors and solids: blues, pinks, reds, maroons, purples, and yellows. These imposing plants can grow 3 ft. tall, and they're very husky, like some portly English country squire. Like many such squires, a few

of them may fit in well with a crowd, but a crowd of them on their own makes sense only in a garden of parklike proportions.

Balloonflower

This flower, *Platycodon*, is related to the campanulas. The reason for this will become obvious to you if you grow this charming and unusual plant. As the deep blue buds swell, the petals stick together, forming blue balloons. Of course, the blossoms finally do open, and the open flowers are lovely, too. This gives you a two-stage treat. Balloonflower also comes in white and pink, but these don't have the impact of the blues.

Solomon's-seal

This North American wildflower, *Polygonatum*, is a member of the lily family. It is a shade lover that produces long, arching shoots from

Purple salvia adds much-needed color in high summer. (Photo by Charles Mann.)

Hen-and-chickens takes care of itself. (Photo by Charles Mann.)

which dangle small, pendulous white bells, followed by dark blue fruits. The flowers have an enchanting perfume, and the arching branches create an interesting effect in deep shade. A giant version of this plant, to 3 ft. tall, makes an excellent addition to a shady background.

Salvia

Salvia, particularly red salvia, is very common in sunny American gardens, highway dividers, shopping-center islands, and other places there is a heavy dose of sun and the institutional mind. But you're not looking for that. You want something interesting and personal, right? Try perennial purple salvia, *Salvia* x *superba* 'East Friesland' or meadow sage. If you have full sun, these 18-in. spikes of intense violet-blue will bloom their heads off all summer. This member of the sage family is not fussy about soil and survives drought very well. It really does need sun, though.

Hen-and-chickens

Also known as *Sempervivum*, this succulent plant is nearly indestructible. (*Sempervivum* translates as "live forever.") The fleshy leaves form little rosettes, which eventually flower. They multiply with vigor, the new rosettes emerging from the base of the plant beneath the leaves much like chicks under a mother hen. After blooming, the original rosette will slowly die, its propagative function fulfilled, to be replaced by the smaller plants.

The flowers of hen-and-chickens are star-shaped in a range of pinks and yellows. There are so many varieties that to be sure of color, you really have to see them in bloom. The leaves can be green, gray, brown, blue, pink, or red. This is a good plant for the rock garden or a stony area. It will thrive where others fail.

Spiderwort

Spiderwort (*Tradescantia*), also known as trinity flower (it has three petals), is an American wildflower partial to shady stream banks. The variety that I grow is *T.* x *andersoniana* 'Zwanenburg Blue', but there are several other native varieties. Most are blue or purple, but it has been bred to produce whites and pinks, too. Spiderwort will grow 2 ft. tall in conditions it likes (partly sunny, damp, but with good drainage). Each flower hangs on its own little stem, making a cluster of buds that looks like a small bunch of green grapes. Like daylilies, the individual flowers last only one day.

Spiderwort is rather common in the country and suburbs but unusual in the city. I suppose conditions are more favorable outside of town. However, it's ideal for any partly shady area with rich soil and water.

Delphiniums

What a stately and elegant plant! I wish I could grow delphiniums, but alas, they need full sun, something I can't provide. The stalks can grow to 6 or 7 ft.—spectacular towers of blue, white, and purple—making them one of the most impressive flowering plants.

Delphiniums are one of the most stately garden plants, sure to grab attention. (Photo by Charles Mann.)

Because delphiniums like cold weather, they do best in the North—Zone 6 and colder. To the south, in Zone 7 and warmer, they are not reliably perennial, but they can be grown as annuals in the cooler seasons. (This should not deter you from trying them if you have full sun. We grow many plants as annuals, so why not try delphiniums?) They need a long period of dormancy in winter and cool nights in summer to be at their best. Some of the most spectacular ones I have seen were grown in Maine.

There are a couple of outstanding strains of tall delphiniums that you should know about: the Pacific Giant strain and the Blackmore & Langdon (B&L) strain. The Pacific Giant strain grows to 7 ft. tall. It has a nice color range, from deep violet to pink to white. The cultivars are named from Arthurian legend, hence 'Astolat', 'King Arthur', 'Galahad', 'Guinevere', and so on. The B&L strain grows 5 to 7 ft. tall in colors ranging from whites to blues to purples. Both strains are proven performers and may bloom the first year.

The tall delphiniums flower in June, and if you remove the old stems after flowering, they usually have another bloom in September. Full sun and rich, deep soil will make them happy, but they should be sheltered from the wind and staked because the stems are so big and heavy that wind and rain may topple them.

There are also short delphiniums for the front of the border that provide intense blues, purples, and lavenders. A newer development is a strain called 'Beverly Hills', which is suited for the more tropical Zones 7 through 10. Plants in this strain come in shades of yellow, salmon, and scarlet. They don't seem very delphinium-like to me, as their glitz is just a little too "Hollywood" for my taste.

CHAPTER 13

High Summer: July, August, and Early September

This is the part of summer when the flowers of the meadow come into their full glory, the time when the Calvary Church garden is awash in black-eyed Susans and when hostas begin to add a tint of lavender and white to the areas thus far dominated by ferns.

THE MAIN COURSE

Hostas

Hostas are members of the lily family and are originally from the Far East. Plant breeders have created many more varieties. Few plants are as useful as hostas. They are usually thought of as good shade plants, but they also do well in areas that get partial sun. Although they're often considered foliage plants, many hosta varieties have lovely lavender or white flowers that are carried on long stems. They work well as ground covers and will choke out weeds very effectively; they quickly become so dense that the weeds can't compete for growing space.

Hosta foliage ranges from yellow to gray-blue to deep blue-green, and many varieties are variegated in tones of gold or cream. Planted in an area they like, hostas will form large colonies. In a small garden, thin them every couple of years, or you soon will have nothing but hostas.

Different species of hostas mix nicely, and if you like this plant, you will want to mix them. This creates visual interest through the texture and color of the leaves. In my garden, the hosta flower stalks begin their upward climb around the first of June, and the different varieties' bloom often extends through August. Some catalogs (see p. 126) offer hosta collections of five or six varieties, an economical way to get started.

Sedum

Sedum is a fleshy-leaved plant that looks as if it would be more at home in the Sonoran Desert than in an eastern garden. But, in fact, it does very well in the North and East. It is a useful source of color in late summer and fall. Bloom develops slowly over a period of weeks. The bloom is actually hundreds of very tiny, long-

SUGGESTED PLANTINGS	
TALLEST	Cimicifuga, tall species lilies, veronicastrum
TALLER	Liatris, monkshood, hybrid lilies, English roses, tall phlox, astilbes
MEDIUM HEIGHT	Black-eyed Susans, nicotiana, cleome, coreopsis
FAIRLY SHORT	Short daylilies, veronica, short astilbes
SHORT	Hostas, impatiens, sedum

THE GARDEN IN HIGH SUMMER

A Ferns
B Astilbe
C Sedum
D Hydrangea
E Hosta
F Toad lily
G Caladiums
H Rhododendron
I Birch tree
J Late lilies
K Climbing rose
L Late monkshood
M Boxwood
N Impatiens
O English rose
P Coreopsis
Q Black-eyed Susans
R Colchicum
S Crab apple
T Alyssum
U Veronicastrum
V Nicotiana
W Ivy

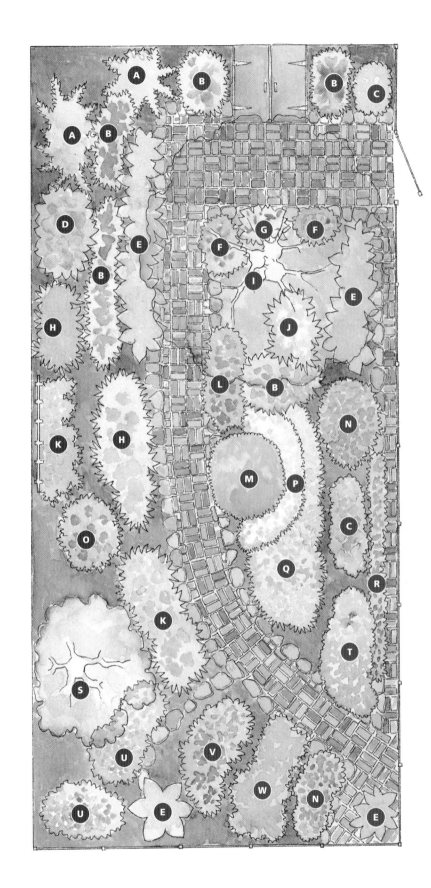

A typical spot where hostas feel at home. (Photo by Derek Fell.)

Sedum dominates this late-summer border. (Photo by Mick Hales.)

lasting flowers. If you are looking for a "no trouble" plant, this is it. I have never had to do anything to mine but watch it grow.

Sedum likes full sun, but it does just fine in partial shade, too. Like peonies, it dies back completely in winter, so don't forget where the plants are and put something else there by mistake. *Sedum telephium* 'Autumn Joy' is a good variety.

Short Daylilies

The shorter members of the daylily tribe make a nice splash of color toward the front of the garden. There are a number of very colorful miniature varieties with stems 20 to 25 in. tall. The varieties in shades of peach and clear yellow are spectacular. The one called 'Stella de Oro' is a superior variety. If you remove the fertilized seedpods from 'Stella de Oro', it may bloom three times in a season, right through October in Zone 6.

Veronica

Veronica is very hardy and reliable. It produces long, conical flower spikes made up of many tiny flowers. The most useful varieties are the blues, because they bloom in late June and July when most of the other blue flowers are gone. In my garden, this is the "yellow period," when the black-eyed Susans are in full flower and the coreopsis is at its best. A little blue is very welcome at this point in the season.

Veronica has no pest I have ever seen and needs little, if any, care. Once every five years, you may have to trim and divide the plants, but you eventually have to divide most perennial plants anyway (see the section on division in Chapter 14 for details). If you deadhead, or cut off, the spent blossoms in July, chances are you'll see another round of bloom before fall.

Astilbes

Among the best sources of late-summer color are astilbes, which range from white to pink to red and purple. They do fine in full sun but better in partial shade because their feathery plumes will hold their color better.

The miniature daylily 'Stella de Oro' blooms three times a year in the author's garden. (Photo by Charles Mann.)

The rare blue of veronica and the feathery plumes of astilbe highlight the late-summer garden. (Photo by Derek Fell.)

Black-eyed Susans blanket the Calvary Church garden in August. (Photo by Brian Coats.)

Astilbes are best planted in groups, where their massed plumes make a grand statement. The blooms last a long time, the tiny flowers opening progressively. Astilbes come in many shapes and sizes. The larger ones are great plants because they endure, and the tall, green-brown fans add a lovely architectural element to the garden. You can leave them standing well

into the winter. But also consider the shorter astilbes. A very small violet-pink variety called *Astilbe chinensis* 'Pumila' is a real charmer. Less than a foot high, its tiny inflorescences cling tightly to the stems, making them look for all the world like little pussy willow catkins. They're a good choice for late-summer color in a tight garden spot.

Astilbes spread by underground runners, and in conditions they like, they will try to take over. This is not a serious problem, as you can just uproot them, but they get started so fast that they can choke out other plants before you know it. Watch for them to come up in the spring, and where you don't want them, pull the new shoots along with the underground runners. It's a good idea to visit your garden often to catch things like this early.

Black-Eyed Susans

Rudbeckia, the yellow varieties at least, have the wonderful old name black-eyed Susan. I know this is impossibly romantic, but I have a vision of some young early American settler naming this native North American species after his lady love.

However it got its name, this plant is a garden mainstay. In the hottest season of the year, black-eyed Susan is at its best, forming a golden blanket over a great swath of garden. It has no significant pests, it self-seeds, and it tends to spread slowly, so it's quite manageable. I recommend this plant highly. You can also interplant it with Canterbury bells (they get along together nicely) so that you will have blue in May and June, followed by sunny yellow in July and part of August. ("What is the special today, waiter?" "Canterbury bells followed by black-eyed Susan, sir." "Thank you. I'll take two!")

Nicotiana

Nicotiana is what its name implies: tobacco—the flowering variety, not the smoking or chewing kind. Most of the varieties I see are on the short side, which can be useful for a compact garden. My real preference, though, lies with

The relaxed nicotiana softens the architectural stiffness of this stony nook. (Photo by Karen Bussolini.)

the old-fashioned 3-ft. varieties (*Nicotiana alata*). I use them for late-summer color in a spot where I grow species tulips in the spring. They don't compete with each other at all. Nicotiana is just getting started by the time the tulip foliage fades. Nicotiana is an annual, but it is also a prolific self-seeder, which means that once you have it, you have it forever. It will produce so many seedlings that you'll need to thin them rather mercilessly, but you can do that in an hour. It's worth it, though. The red, pink, and white flowers look like angels' trumpets.

Cleome

Another great self-seeder and a staple of the late-summer garden is cleome. This tall-growing plant has a top tuft of flowers reminiscent of phlox, surrounded by long "whiskers" (actually seedpods) that make them look a little like spiders (and are the source of their other name, spider flower). The subtle shades of lavender, white, and pink can continue until frost, making this a valuable plant.

Cleome is not fussy, doesn't mind drought, and doesn't have any significant pests. The seedpods burst open in the fall and plant next year's crop, making it a perfect plant: It does all

Cleome is a self-seeding wonder that appears every August. (Photo by Paddy Wales.)

the work, and you do nothing. If you do want to move cleome around, it transplants very successfully. The transplants will look droopy for an afternoon, but with a little water they will be fine on the morrow. The many seeds are also easy to harvest if you want to give some to your friends.

If you want cleome and nicotiana to self-seed successfully, avoid applying winter mulch where they grow. It will retard the germination of the seeds, and you'll lose one of these plants' best attributes: no need for planting.

Coreopsis

Coreopsis is easy to grow and will present you with a mass of golden flowers from midsummer until fall. Look for *Coreopsis verticillata* 'Moonbeam', which Wayside Gardens rates as one of the 10 best perennials of all time. It has creamy yellow daisylike flowers and delicate, ferny foliage. It looks best backed up by something dark, such as evergreens, which will make the $1\frac{1}{2}$-in. flowers stand out to good effect.

In full sun, coreopsis will flower all summer. In partial shade, mine don't bloom until July, but then they go nonstop till frost. They are great for a cutting garden because the more you cut them, the more they bloom. If you don't want cut flowers, be sure to deadhead them anyway to keep the flowers coming. Coreopsis is heat and drought tolerant. It spreads by underground runners to form clumps, but it will not take over your garden like a weed.

There are some double varieties, such as 'Early Sunrise', an excellent plant. The pink species *C. rosea* doesn't look like coreopsis to me.

Liatris

The spiky plant liatris, also known as blazing star, grows up to 5 ft. tall. The flower clusters are made up of $\frac{1}{2}$-in. florets in shades of pink or white that open, oddly enough, from the top of the spike down. Liatris likes full sun or partial shade and average soil and moisture, although it will not live in standing water. It has no significant pests or diseases.

Coreopsis, or tickseed, is a reliable performer in late summer. (Photo by Derek Fell.)

Liatris is great for summer color when spring bloomers have faded. (Photo by Charles Mann.)

Because liatris is so tall, most people grow it in the back of the border. (Many folks have such a military mind about placement: everything in ranks and rows.) I put a white one in the middle of a stand of irises in the front of my garden. The irises finish blooming in June; the liatris blooms in July, bringing interest to a spot that would otherwise be kind of a dud for most of the year. Liatris blooms up until frost.

Monkshood

Monkshood, or aconitum, is so named because the individual flowers look like little hoods covering the tall stems. They are a good source of color during the oppressive days of August, the blue variety being the most cooling and stunningly beautiful, but there are also yellow and white species. At 48 in., *Aconitum carmichaelii* is a stately plant in medium blue and is quite eye-catching planted behind yellow black-eyed Susans. *A. lamarckii* is a soft yellow species, also 40 to 48 in. tall, but it will need to be planted

Monkshood seems appropriate for a church garden, but has some deadly characteristics. (Photo by Charles Mann.)

closer to the front of a border, as it is not as assertive as its blue cousins.

My favorite, and the most useful in my garden, is *A. henryi* 'Sparks Variety', which makes a stunning background at about 6 ft. tall. It is a deep blue violet and very striking, because it blooms late in the year when blues in the garden are scarce.

Monkshood is not difficult to grow, doing well in partial shade or full sun, but it does need reliable moisture during dry spells and will not grow where there is standing water or puddles. It is susceptible to powdery mildew. An occasional dousing with a fungicide, like benomyl, will help a lot.

Monkshood is also known as wolfsbane. According to legend, during the Middle Ages the people of Europe used to tie the plant up in slabs of meat in order to poison wolves that were preying on livestock. You can believe what you want, but it's my opinion that meat was so scarce in medieval Europe that the people would have been fighting the wolves over it, poison or not. Plants of the *Aconitum* genus *are* poisonous, though, so if you have small children or pets about, you'd better not plant monkshood.

Lilies

Lilies are a large genus of plants native to woodland borders in the temperate zone of the Northern Hemisphere around the world. They are among the most rewarding garden plants and, if carefully selected, will give you blooms from May to September. That's a long time!

A mixture of lily types can provide all-summer bloom. (Photo by Charles Mann.)

Their colors range from pure white through pastel shades to deep red. (Sorry, no blues, although some of the newest strains have a distinctly violet cast.) Though most are shorter, some grow up to an astounding 7 ft. tall. For this reason, you will want them farther back in your border, although they also work very well as an architectural accent. Lilies don't seem to mind being interplanted with other perennials, as long as you don't disturb them. A lily bulb will produce for many years, so choose your planting site with care.

I recommend that you try all sorts of lilies; there are almost enough for every day in summer. Try some of the lilies that bear the most resemblance to their wild forebears, such as *Lilium martagon*, a pink-to-purple Turk's-cap lily with deeply recurved petals. It does well in shade and is tolerant of a variety of soil conditions. You will not want this one for a dinner table centerpiece, though, as it has an unpleasant aroma.

Roses

The everblooming English roses and the climbing roses are just fine for city gardens. There are many devotees of hybrid tea roses, and I guess if I had more space, I would grow them. But they need a lot of room and care. They are also quite susceptible to diseases. English roses have many fine, full blossoms (some bloom all summer). They also are not subject to contracting every disease within a 100-mile radius and are reliably winter hardy with mulch. Some varieties only grow to 3 ft., so these are perfect for smaller gardens. I have one called 'Fair Bianca' that blooms into November!

Climbing roses, grown over walls, fences, and the like, are a very effective backdrop for the garden. There are many well-proven varieties, such as 'Blaze', that are practically indestructible. I have a light pink climber in the back of my garden that grows against the brownstone wall of the church to great effect. It is so old that no one remembers its name. During a series of major snowstorms, the weight of the ice on the rose broke four main stems and I was afraid it was a goner. Yet the following summer, it bloomed as if nothing had happened.

The world of roses is so vast and complex that it takes total dedication to thread one's way through it. Rose people are called rosarians (not to be confused with Rosicrucians, who are members of the Ancient Mystic Order Rosae Crucis). I like roses, but I am neither Rosicrucian nor rosarian, so I will suggest only a few types, such as the roses of hybridizer David Austin. These are vigorous versions of the English rose that bloom nearly all summer. Another winner is the Meidiland landscape rose from France, which is a very hardy shrub of medium stature that is great for hedges. Landscape roses require little care and are disease resistant—good qualities to me.

There are many books devoted exclusively to roses. If you are interested in their culture, try to find a book written by a rosarian for laypeople, not for other rosarians. Rosarians speak to each other in a language that resembles Botanical Latin in form but refers exclusively to roses.

Phlox

Phlox is a familiar and frequent sight in older gardens throughout the eastern United States. Your grandmother, no doubt, grew phlox, and so did her mother. Most phlox species grow 3 to 4 ft. tall and tend to be bushy. If your garden is tiny, you may not want to devote that much space to phlox, but if you can afford the room, it's worth it. Phlox comes in many colors, so you can match just about any color scheme you want. The plants need rich soil, some sun, lots of water, and little else to present you with big heads of fragrant flowers. They make wonderful cut flowers for your home.

Phlox was the mainstay of your mother's garden; it would look good in yours, too. (Photo by Derek Fell.)

The blooms of cimicifuga resemble bottle brushes and are beloved by bees. (Photo by Janet Loughrey.)

Cimicifuga

Cimicifuga is not a common plant in American gardens, but it's gaining popularity. And no wonder! It is one of the most useful tall-growing plants for the perennial garden. Cimicifuga blooms in late June, July, and sometimes August. The blooms resemble nothing so much as a white bottle brush on a very long handle (the stems can reach 6 ft. tall). These long plumes wave gently in the slightest wind and make for a background plant that generates a lot of interest.

Cimicifuga is very hardy and spreads by both seed and underground runners. If you have given cimicifuga a place it likes (it's not that picky), it will "go forth and multiply." This is only a slightly pesky habit, as it is pretty easy to remove. If you don't pull it up, though, its dense foliage will kill whatever else is there. I have seen it kill a nice stand of irises in only one season.

Cimicifuga is also known as bugbane. This seems to be a misnomer, as it is very attractive to bees and other nectar-seeking insects.

The Plague: Purple Loosestrife

I am plagued by a weed—or wildflower, depending on personal opinion—that I have very mixed feelings about: purple loosestrife (*Lythrum salicaria*). This plant is actually quite lovely. I have seen entire fields of nothing but purple loosestrife in the Northeast. It's a glorious sight, but this profusion is also indicative of its problem. It is very prolific. It will take over anywhere, and if you don't constantly monitor your garden for seedlings, you will soon have *only* purple loosestrife. I would like to keep one or two at the back of the garden, as they are so lovely, but you can't have one or two. With purple loosestrife, it's all or nothing. Most seedsmen will not sell this plant anymore because it is now considered by most to be an obnoxious weed.

Purple loosestrife is beautiful from afar, but in your garden, it's the worst sort of pest. (Photo by Charles Mann.)

I'm gradually replacing my purple loosestrife with a much better behaved plant called veronicastrum, or Culver's root. It has the same growing habits, and the foliage is almost indistinguishable from purple loosestrife's. Instead of purple spikes, it has white ones. Best of all, veronicastrum does not appear to be subject to the rapacious land-grabbing tendencies of its greedy cousin.

Veronicastrum will grow 4 to 5 ft. tall, which makes it just right for a background planting. The slender white spikes bloom from late July into September. It is reliably hardy and rather elegant looking. I'd like to see this plant in a lot more gardens.

If you summer your houseplants outdoors, be sure to check them for unwanted guests before bringing them indoors for the winter. (Photo by Derek Fell.)

CHAPTER 14

Houseplants: The End of Summer Vacation

I TAKE MANY OF OUR HOUSEPLANTS across the street to the garden for the summer. This vacation does them a lot of good. Exposure to the outdoors eliminates pests indigenous to the indoors, where they have no natural predators. Outdoors, nature seems to play them off each other. Things don't usually get out of hand except for an occasional plague of aphids or the annual return of the Japanese beetle. When it's time to bring the plants back in for the winter, I know I'm going to have some unwanted guests—guests that will multiply rapidly in the security of the indoor environment.

PESTS: THE WORST OFFENDERS

The two biggest pest problems you will face indoors will probably be scale insects and spider mites. They are tenacious and hard to see. They also do their dirty work quickly. A plant will often be in the throes of death before you know it has a problem.

Scale Insects

Scale insects are tricky because in the younger state, when they are mobile, they are very hard to see—little, semi-transparent brown or tan oblong spots that look as if they could be part of the plant. This, of course, is part of the insect's

survival strategy. Even though they are mobile at this point, you will not see them move. It is a slow process.

The adults affix themselves to one spot and form a hard shell. This shell can be a small brown hemisphere from 2 to 10 mm in size. (If it looks fuzzy, like a little piece of lint, it's a mealybug. Treat it exactly the same way as scale.) The trouble is you will almost never see the insects at this stage outdoors because some predator will have had them for dinner. Only indoors will they become noticeable. You may see the adults, or you may notice a sticky substance that they exude on the leaves. If you look closely at the undersides of the leaves and at the stems, you will see the younger insects. I have seen scale on fig trees, jade plants, and citrus plants.

For plants you suspect might be harboring scale, gently rub the leaves and stems with rubbing alcohol on a cotton ball. If the plant is infested with young scale insects, you'll see them on the cotton. Remove as many as you can, then spray the plant, especially the young leaves and stems, with insecticidal soap. Remember to spray the undersides of the leaves, too.

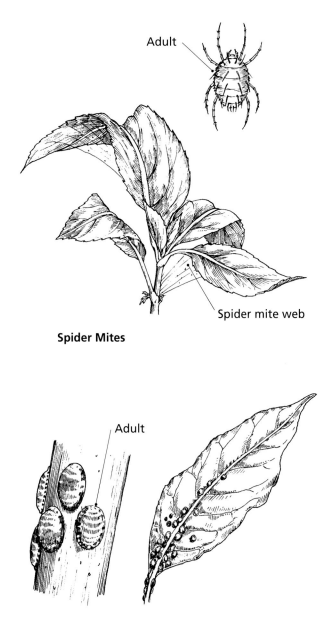

Adult

Spider mite web

Spider Mites

Adult

Scale Insects

Spider Mites

Spider mites are almost invisible. You may notice that the leaves around the crowns of the plant are shriveling and turning brown. If you look closely, you will see that the crowns are enveloped in very thin webs. You may need a magnifying glass to see the tiny insects that are sucking the plant dry. Alternatively, you can mist the crowns to make the webs stand out. This insect loves impatiens and is always a problem when you bring cuttings of the plant indoors to root. It also finds leaves of citrus plants particularly toothsome.

You can control spider mites by rinsing the plants with a stiff spray of water. Don't forget the undersides of the leaves, which are a favorite haunt of both spider mites and scale insects. Better yet, make a weak solution of soapy water (a mild dishwashing liquid or soap flakes are fine, but laundry detergents are too strong). Wrap the pot and base of the plant in plastic to keep the soil from falling out as you invert the plant. Carefully dip the plant into the soapy water and swish the leaves around. You do not need to rinse the plant, as residual soap is a deterrent to spider mites.

THE ISOLATION WARD

Even if you have treated your houseplants outdoors, you may still see pests inside. There may have been some eggs left under a leaf, or they may come in on another plant. You never know what surprises a greenhouse plant may harbor either, so it is a good idea to isolate the new plant for a couple of weeks to see what may develop. It is easier to treat one plant than a whole household.

PESTICIDES

Insecticidal soap is a mild pesticide with a short life—that is, it won't stay poisonous very long and can be used on vegetables up to the day before harvest. If you have children or pets, this is the only insecticide I'd recommend for indoor plants. I can't use pesticides such as malathion, Orthene, or Sevin indoors because of our cats, who have been known to chomp on a leaf occasionally. These pesticides are not only contact poisons, but they are also systemics. The plant will absorb them into its system through the roots and leaves. (You may see the word *systemic* on the label.) Then the whole plant is poisonous, and any bug that bites it is going to die. Unfortunately, it can also be fatal to anything else that takes a bite, such as a cat or a kid. So don't use these on any houseplant if you have children or pets, even if it is outdoors for the summer. There is really no way of knowing how long the poison will remain in the plant's system.

Most of the time, high-powered pesticides like malathion, Isotox, Orthene, and Sevin are unnecessary for the flower garden. Using them is sort of like dropping an atomic bomb to get rid of a pesky mouse. These pesticides kill the beneficial insects (bees, ladybugs, and so on) along with the pests. Most of the time in the garden, it is better to sacrifice a little foliage so that the good insects may go on living. Of course, there will be times, such as when a horde of aphids descends on your daylilies, when you will have to resort to the bomb, or you will have no daylilies that year.

Check susceptible plants for scale indoors. Include succulents such as the jade plant but not cacti. Look closely for the immature insects.

You will see them better on a stem than on a leaf. Also look for the adults. If you see just a few, remove them by hand with a cotton swab dipped in rubbing alcohol. Check every couple of days for a resurgence. If you have a large scale invasion, put the plant in the bathtub, soak it with insecticidal soap, and isolate it for several days.

Look for the tiny webs of spider mites in the crowns of tender plants. Spider mites bother only plants that they can penetrate. You will not see spider mites hanging around a jade plant or a cactus. If you see webs, dunk the plant in soapy water again. You may have to repeat this several times at weekly intervals to get them all.

Spider mites lay their eggs on the leaves, so some plant hygiene is beneficial. Remove any shriveled or dead leaves from the plant before washing it and remove any fallen leaves from inside the pot or around it. Wash off the outside of the pot as well.

THE REVERSE PLAY

Curiously enough, some plants will thrive indoors or out. I have a friend who potted up a rather large hosta and brought it indoors, where it still is today, several years later. I was sure it would wither and die, but it is apparently quite happy on her dining room table. If you try this, be sure to treat the plant just like your houseplants you bring indoors. It will be hosting the same sort of unwanted guests.

Miscanthus sinensis is one of the best winter grasses because it's showy and hardy. (Photo by Derek Fell.)

CHAPTER 15

The Last Hurrah: Late September and October

BY THE MIDDLE OF SEPTEMBER, as the heat diminishes in the temperate zones (see the USDA Plant Hardiness Zone Map on p. 131), the garden begins to wind down. However, there's a lot left to look forward to. The cimicifuga and astilbes may still be in bloom, and if not, there are the seedpods on the long stems of the former and the green-brown fans of the latter. Even though there is no startling color to enjoy, the shapes and textures of fading summer plants provide the architectural elements that are so important to the winter garden landscape. Winter is when you see the interesting shapes of the stems that are hidden during the growing season. You will begin to see the curiously gnarled stems of *Corylus avellana* 'Contorta', also known as Harry Lauder's walking stick. (Harry Lauder was an old-time Scottish comic.) Although this shrub has hanging catkins in spring, it is grown primarily for its winter interest. So, too, are the red twig and yellow twig dogwoods and willows.

Ornamental grasses also provide fall and winter interest and are becoming very popular with those who have some space. If you are a small-space gardener, you probably can't afford a big mound of grass 9 ft. high and 18 ft. around, such as pampas grass. But there are several smaller varieties that might merit your consideration, such as *Miscanthus sinensis* 'Gracillimus'. About

4 ft. high, it forms feathery heads that turn a beautiful gold in winter. It looks great against a white fence, snow, or dark brick or stone. You will want to put this in a place where it won't block your view of summer flowers.

If you're very interested in these winter shapes, I'd recommend that you read Rosemary Verey's lavishly illustrated *The Garden in Winter* (Little, Brown & Co., 1988), which is, to my mind, the definitive work on the colors and textures of the season.

FALL BLOOMERS

Some sedum varieties will still be blooming well into fall and so will some late-blooming hostas. Your most reliable color, though, will continue to come from the impatiens. See what marvelous plants they are? I have one patch planted where they get six hours of sun a day and another in almost total shade, thus forming a foreground for red caladiums, which like no sun

SUGGESTED PLANTINGS	
TALL	Cimicifuga, tall astilbes
MEDIUM HEIGHT	Resurrection lily, asters, Japanese toad lily
SHORT	Colchicum, fall-blooming crocuses, late hostas, sedum, impatiens

Ornamental grasses give a garden fall and winter texture. (Photo by Karen Bussolini.)

at all. Both patches bloom into November! Beyond the hangers-on from summer and early fall, there are several tall-blooming plants for those wise enough to plan ahead.

Colchicum

By this time of year, you will not find any more flats of annuals with which to fill in bare spots. But there the sagacious gardener will have planted colchicum. Colchicum looks like giant crocuses, although the two are not related. The flowers appear without leaves, rising straight up out of the ground with no apparent stem. Some are an astonishing 12 in. tall. They can be white, lilac, or pink and look great along the foot of a wall or fence. If your garden is visible from a heavily trafficked street like mine, they will draw a lot of spectators.

The leaves of colchicum grow in spring and early summer and are not that attractive. You must let them grow until they turn yellow, though, or the bulb may not bloom. You can plant colchicum among irises or other taller plants to distract attention away from the yellowing leaves. I have mine at the base of some tall bearded irises.

Plant colchicum as soon as you receive the bulbs. Otherwise, there's a good chance that these big bulbs will bloom in the bag, and that's not good for the colchicum. You will often see pictures in catalogs of a colchicum bulb blooming on a windowsill without benefit of planting. But beware: If you do this, you can kiss your colchicum good-bye. It will not survive the experience. This plant is expensive, so you won't want that to happen.

Colchicum takes its name from the ancient city of Colchis on the Black Sea. During the Dark and Middle Ages, Colchis was the world's poison mart, its back streets rife with "pharmacists" who had a poison for every occasion. One of these was colchicine, a distillate of colchicum. Today colchicine is an important substance in the genetic manipulation of plants. It doubles the number of chromosomes present in the next generation, creating a more vigorous plant.

Fall-Blooming Crocuses

There are a number of lovely varieties of fall-blooming crocuses, virtually all in the pink to purple range. These can be planted with the colchicum if you want to fill in the display (crocuses are a lot cheaper than colchicum). If you can get them planted by the middle of September, they will bloom in a month. It's a great last shot of color in the autumn garden.

Crocus sativus, the saffron crocus, is one of the fall bloomers. It is the source of the spice saffron, which is the stigma of the flower, the part that receives the pollen grains. Crocus stigmas are small, so you will need to grow a lot to flavor your paella. The saffron crocus also exists in an unusual, and consequently expensive, white variety. Legend has it that the Pythia, the priestess and oracle at Delphi, would present these rare blossoms as an offering to Pythian Apollo, the inspiration for her insights into the future. She would then proceed with her inscrutable, and no doubt drug-induced, prophecies, which were the last word in the classical period of the Greek world.

The poisoner's favorite—colchicum—is also the gardener's. (Photo by Mick Hales.)

Aster x frikartii 'Monch' has been declared by one top authority to be one of the six best plants in the world. (Photo by Derek Fell.)

Resurrection Lily

Lycoris squamigera, resurrection lily, is a spectacular plant for this time of year, or earlier in some parts of the country. (I suspect that we think most of the plants that bloom in the fall are spectacular because there are so few, relatively speaking.) These bulbs produce moderately attractive straplike foliage in the early summer that disappears in July. Then, in late

August or September, 2- to 3-ft. stems arise, bearing pink lily-like flowers. They are nothing less than fabulous planted en masse. Eight to 10 or more produce the best effect. They may take a year to settle in before they bloom, and they need sun and well-drained soil. A little top-dressing of phosphate fertilizer in the spring is good for them. There are other types of fall-blooming lycoris, but they are not hardy in Zone 6, and I wouldn't trust them in Zone 7, either. If you live in Zone 8, give them a try.

Asters

The aster is certainly the queen of the fall garden and well worth more attention than she gets in the United States. This plant is an American native, growing wild in a wide range of habitats. Asters are no trouble to grow, and they perform well as long as they get plenty of sun and water. They tend to grow tall, a problem easily solved by pinching them back. Or you could plant dwarf asters, which bloom quite as prolifically as their taller relatives.

One of the very best asters is *Aster* x *frikartii* 'Monch', developed in the 1920s by the well-known Frikart Nursery in Switzerland. A famous plantsman, Graham Stuart Thomas, called this "one of the six best plants." He didn't mean one of the six best fall plants; he meant one of the six best plants of all time! It grows about 2½ ft. tall and, under the right conditions, produces light blue flowers all summer and fall.

Japanese Toad Lily

Well, I have never seen any toads around mine, not that I'd mind. Toads are such useful creatures, and any gardener is lucky to have one take up residence in his or her garden. (One toad can devour pounds of destructive insects in a season.) But Japanese toad lily (*Tricyrtis*) is an unusual late bloomer, putting forth 1-in. flowers of a lilac or amethyst hue in midfall. It loves damp, humus-rich conditions, needs practically

The Japanese toad lily blooms when all else has gone to bed for the winter. (Photo by Janet Loughrey.)

no light at all, and blooms until it's out of breath or until frost arrives, whichever comes first.

My Japanese toad lily grows under a birch, away from the street and closed in by astilbes, tall lilies, and cimicifuga. I hardly ever see it until all the other things die back and the birch loses some of its leaves. Then the stalwart little toad lily displays a hundred or more blossoms that look like miniature orchids. This plant is a valuable addition to a long-blooming garden, requires absolutely no care, and will repay your studied neglect by thriving for many years and bursting into joyful bloom every September.

BLACK IN THE BACK

In late October or early November, the tall stems and seedpods of cimicifuga will cease to be attractive architectural elements by turning completely black, as though hit by some disastrous blight. At this point, it's best to cut them down and dispose of the remains, particularly as the unsightly foliage will draw attention away from whatever flowers may still be blooming. Take heart, though. They will come back stronger than ever next year.

Something similar happens to the astilbe foliage a little later, and those stems should come down, too, in preparation for your final garden chores of the year.

Winter allows you to see the bare bones of your garden. (Photo by Derek Fell.)

CHAPTER 16
Putting the Garden to Bed: Late November and Early December

BY LATE NOVEMBER or early December, you will probably get the first frost in Zone 6. This will kill the leaves and stems of all but the toughest plants. The sedum will last a while longer, and if you have the right conditions to grow the Lenten rose (*Helleborus orientalis*), you will see its evergreen foliage all winter, presaging its very early bloom (January to March). But for most of us, it is cleanup time.

Gardens are a lot like Thanksgiving. After a great Thanksgiving feast, it's tempting to just sit back and relax. Someone, however, has to do the dishes. It would be easier to throw them out, but then next Thanksgiving you wouldn't have the beautiful china upon which to serve the feast.

WINTERIZING THE SMALL-SPACE GARDEN

Winterizing a small garden means cleaning, cutting back, mulching, dividing, and protecting.

Cleaning

Cleanup not only makes your garden space look better, but it also gets rid of pests and diseases. Old leaves, stems, flower heads, and such provide shelter for insects, insect eggs, and disease organisms. If you don't want to see their renaissance next year, get rid of this debris. If you are maintaining a compost pile, dump the debris there. Be sure to discard any obviously diseased foliage. If you don't compost, bag up the debris and put it out on leaf collection days or take it to your local landfill.

Cutting Back

After a frost has killed the tops, cut your herbaceous perennial plants, such as peonies, back to the ground. Use your clippers or pruners to do this because pulling on the stems may harm the roots. You may want to use a label stake to mark the spot where the plant grows so that you don't plant something else there in your early-spring zeal. (This is remarkably easy to do.)

Roses should be cut back to 18 to 20 in. after a hard freeze. Be sure to collect all the debris around the plant, as roses are very susceptible to diseases, such as botrytis, which can winter over on dead leaves.

Mulching

Apply a mulch such as shredded bark to a depth of 2 to 3 in. The purpose of winter mulch is not to keep the plants warm; they need the cold weather for their period of dormancy. Instead, the mulch prevents damage from alternate freezing and thawing, which can heave the plants right out of the ground, particularly those that are newly planted. Apply mulch after there has been a hard freeze, about 20°F. The mulch will help keep the soil around the plant frozen during winter warm spells.

Some plants, however, should not be mulched. *Heuchera*, for instance, remains evergreen. It does not like its crown covered. Columbine will not send up shoots in the spring if it is totally covered. Do not mulch areas where you have self-seeding annuals. Two to 3 in. of mulch will prevent their seeds from germinating. Do not put mulch directly against tree trunks or the bases of shrubs. Mulch retains moisture and causes rot in woody plants. Each plant has its own preference about this, so if you're not sure, consult another reference work, such as *The Compleat Gardener* by Lois Wilson (Hawthorne Books, 1970).

Heap mulch around the bases of roses. For really cold areas with drying winter winds, it's a good idea to cover roses completely. Here's how: Make a cylinder out of burlap, hardware cloth (wire mesh), or chicken wire wrapped around stakes. Hardware cloth is best because it is heavier and stands up to the wind. Put this around the plant and fill it with tree leaves or evergreen boughs. This will allow the plant to breathe while protecting it from direct icy blasts. Remove this arrangement in early spring so that new canes will form.

Dividing

Many perennial plants will eventually develop into a big, crowded clump. Others, like irises, will form huge rhizomes underground. Both these circumstances retard blooming, and division is necessary.

Plants such as coreopsis, daisies, astilbes, and even hostas will tend to multiply in tight clumps. When this happens, it creates so much competition among the individual plants that they devote all their resources to obtaining nourishment and water, to the detriment of the flowers. You will have to dig up these clumps with your garden fork and divide them into a manageable size. Use the fork to break each clump into several pieces and replant them apart. In a small space, you may not be able to replant them all, but what you don't use, you can give away to friends with gardens. Most gardeners love to get divisions. I have gotten some very nice daylilies and heuchera this way. Water the replanted divisions deeply.

Protecting Roses in Winter

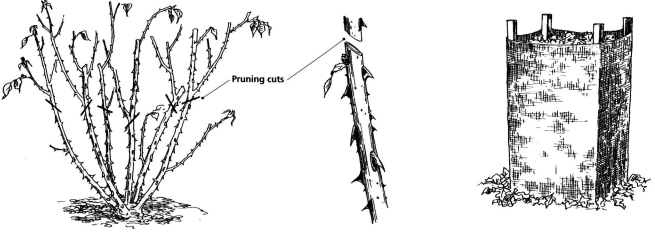

Pruning cuts

1. Prune roses back by a third to a half after leaf drop in the fall. Remove any dead or dying wood and remove debris from around the plant to prevent disease.

2. If buds are visible, make pruning cuts ¼ inch above an outward-facing bud.

3. To protect roses from drying winter winds, make a cylinder of burlap, chicken wire, or hardware cloth and fill it with leaves or evergreen boughs. Remove in early spring.

Dividing Perennials

1. When plants are dormant in late fall, dig them up with a garden fork.

2. Using the fork, break the plants apart into several clumps.

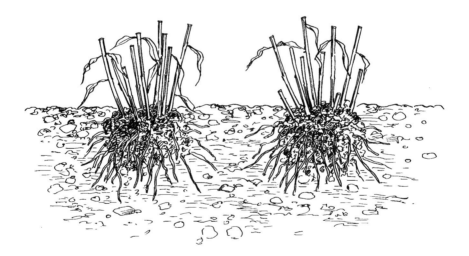

3. Replant the clumps at the same soil level as they were planted previously and water deeply. If foliage is tall, cut it down to prevent wind damage.

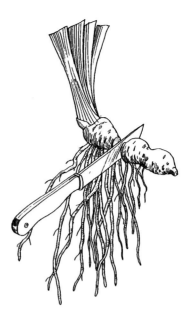

2. Cut away the excess rhizome, leaving about 1 in. attached to the leaves, and discard it. Trim the leaves to a 5-in. fan. Dust the cut rhizome with horticultural sulfur or fungicide to prevent infection.

1. In the fall, dig up overgrown iris rhizomes.

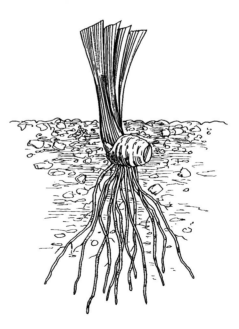

3. Replant the fans with rhizome 1 in. below soil surface. Water deeply and repeat weekly until plants are established.

Irises are a different matter. Over a period of several years, they will develop very large and long rhizomes—the part that stores starch. It's my theory that the irises have so much food stored up that they get lazy. Since there is no urgent need to reproduce, they don't direct their efforts toward flowering.

You need to dig them up with your garden fork and remove the greater part of the rhizomes. You will be surprised how big these rhizomes can get. I dug up one that had grown around in a circle that was as big as an automobile steering wheel. The plants don't need *that* much food.

As you dig them, cut the rhizomes back to 1 in. and cut the leaves back to 4 to 5 in. so that you have just a small fan. This is for two reasons: First, the long, swordlike leaves require too much energy from the small portion of the rhizome that is left, and second, if you don't trim them, the plants will be top-heavy and fall over, pulling the rhizomes out of the soil.

Set the trimmed plants aside until you finish digging and throw the old rhizomes away. Allow the cut portion of each rhizome to dry off, then dust the area with powdered sulfur (available at garden stores) and replant with the rhizome just under the soil's surface. Water well and wait for spring.

Protecting
Depending on where you live, there are certain protective measures to undertake, both before and during the winter months.

Discourage Unwelcome Winter Visitors
If you live in the country, you may have mice, deer, or rabbits to contend with. You can cover favorite deer food with netting. This is available at garden stores or through many catalogs (see p. 126). Netting has a cosmetic advantage over wire mesh and chicken wire because you can't see it from a distance. Use tree wrap to protect young trees and shrubs from mice and rabbits. Some repellents also can be effective and won't harm children or pets. Ask your nursery what is most effective in your area.

Prevent Drying and Breakage Winter winds are very drying and have a deleterious effect on many evergreens. To minimize this, water evergreens deeply in the fall, up until the time the ground freezes. For smaller plants, an antidesiccant spray helps. This puts a coating on evergreen leaves and needles that helps prevent moisture loss.

If you have snow, sweep it off the evergreen branches to prevent breakage. If you have an ice storm, just wait for a thaw. The process of removing ice can cause breakage.

Dig Up Tender Perennials Some perennial plants, such as tuberoses, gladiolus, and dahlias, are not hardy in the North. The bulbs should be dug up and stored for the winter. Allow them to dry in the sun until the foliage withers, then store the bulbs in a cool, dry place. A light dusting of horticultural sulfur will prevent most diseases of bulbs during storage. Next spring, replant them.

The hellebores are among the first plants to bloom. (Photo by Charles Mann.)

CHAPTER 17
A Spring Preview

SO, WHAT DOES A GARDENER DO in the deepness of winter? If you've been gardening for a few years, you will probably be knee deep in catalogs by the middle of December. (See p. 126 for catalogs.) I confess to spending most of my garden budget on fall plantings, but I really enjoy getting the spring books when nothing is blooming. Or is it?

THE HELLEBORES

If you want to treat yourself to something really nice in January or February, try the Christmas rose, *Helleborus niger,* or the Lenten rose, *H. orientalis.* The Christmas rose often will bloom in late December and January in milder areas. It is a hardy evergreen plant that loves shade. Its white blossoms are very long-lived, often lasting through spring and darkening to a rosy color as they age. There is also a variety called *H. viridis,* which has bright green flowers. I think it's hideous, but some gardeners like it.

Many experienced gardeners have no luck with the Christmas rose. It lives for a couple of years, never blooms, and inexplicably dies. The picture is pretty, but the reviews are bad.

The Lenten rose, however, is easy to grow. It blooms just a little later, as the name implies. It is also evergreen and has cup-shaped flowers that range from nearly white to dusty rose with some green undertones. A grouping of three of these plants looks very nice in a shady corner even when flowering is over, as the evergreen foliage is rather handsome.

The exact meaning of the ancient name *helleborus* has been lost in time, but it is thought to mean something like "food to kill." I'm sure a distillate from the roots of the hellebores was right there on the shelf beside colchicine in the poison boutiques of Colchis. Exercise the same care with the hellebores as you would with monkshood. They are quite poisonous.

STARTING SEEDS

In addition to perusing the spring flower books during the winter, you might try your hand at starting some seeds just for fun. To my mind, it's not worth the trouble to start common bedding plants from seed. They are cheap to buy in flats, and the effort spent on them is wasted.

However, many perennial plants that last for years, and houseplants such as the rather expensive Kaffir lily, are easily grown from seed. Even though I had to wait 6 years for my Kaffir lilies to bloom, for the past 12 years they have rewarded my patience twice a year with flower heads of perhaps a dozen 1-in. bright orange flowers with yellow throats. And I'm glad I didn't spend what the catalogs charge for

1. Fill a flat with soilless potting mix.

2. Place the flat in water so that the mix will absorb water from the bottom.

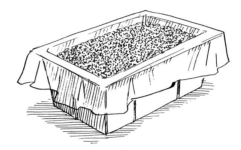

3. Sprinkle seeds evenly over the surface and cover them with a shallow layer of milled sphagnum moss. Cover the flat with plastic wrap and place it in indirect light.

4. When seedlings emerge, uncover the flat and place it in bright indirect light. Be sure you keep it slightly moist.

5. When the second set of leaves emerges, gently remove each plant from the flat with a small spoon or Popsicle stick and plant it in potting soil.

5-year-old plants. (Believe it or not, there is a very rare form of Kaffir lily with yellow flowers currently priced at over $900 each!)

Other valuable and relatively easy perennial plants you can start from seed are columbine, asters, campanulas, and daylilies. It will take the daylilies a couple of years to reach blooming size, but when plants go for over $30 each, it's worth the wait.

Each plant has its own needs for germination. Some need warmth; some need freezing; some need scarification (cutting of the seed coat). Any seedsman you order from will provide directions for proper germination. Most plants don't need any special treatment.

Use a Soilless Mix

In my opinion, the best medium for starting seeds is a soilless mix. This is because such mixes don't contain a lot of undesirable stuff, such as weeds, insects, and diseases that thrive in soil. A soilless mix will likely be made up of various media, including vermiculite, perlite, sphagnum moss, and bark, and it may contain some nutrients as well. You can buy these mixes from various seed houses (Park Seed's mix is exceptionally fine; see p. 127), or you can make one yourself.

To make your own mix, combine two parts vermiculite with one part shredded sphagnum moss in a metal or heatproof ceramic container. Bake it in the oven at 200° F for one hour to kill any mold that may be in the medium. Then fill a plastic flat with drainage holes about three-quarters full with the mix. Flats are available at garden centers and through some catalogs. Park has a nice selection (see p. 127).

Plant the Seeds

Gently place the flat in water so that the mix will absorb moisture from the bottom. When the soilless mix appears to be soaked, drain the flat and then sprinkle the seeds over the surface. Gently cover the seeds with a light dusting of milled sphagnum moss. Some seeds, such as those of begonias, are so small and dustlike that they don't need the covering, but most do. Cover the flat with plastic wrap to keep in the moisture, then put it in a warm place with indirect light.

If the seeds are large enough to handle, you might opt to start them in Styrofoam blocks. These contain a number of individual holes that you fill with the starting mix. The advantage to these blocks is that the individual seedlings can stay right there until the roots fill the holes. Then you just push them out and plant them in larger containers.

Monitor the Flat

Check the flat for moisture regularly. If you think it's dry, water it again from the bottom. When the seedlings appear, uncover the flat and gradually move the flat to bright light.

Check the seedbed regularly for damping-off, a fungus that destroys seedlings at the base of the stem—prevalent when the soil is cold and wet. It looks like a fine, white fuzz. If it appears, dip the flat into a solution of some mild fungicide, such as Benlate or benomyl, and uncover it to reduce the moisture content in the air.

Transplant the Seedlings

When the seedlings emerge, you will see only their seed leaves. Place the flat in bright indirect light, remove the plastic wrap, and wait for the true leaves, the second set, to appear. When they do, you may gently remove the seedlings with a small spoon or Popsicle stick and move the plant to a small pot. Be very careful not to damage the young plant's stem, or it's curtains for the seedling. You can now plant it in a potting mixture (see Chapter 9).

Feed the seedlings with a water-soluble fertilizer on a regular schedule. They will not need any plant food until the second set of leaves appears, since the seed leaves contain enough nourishment.

A classic mixed border. (Photo by Karen Bussolini.)

CHAPTER 18
Some Reflections

IF YOU ARE HOOKED on flower gardening after your first year, you will find many other plants to try in succeeding seasons, and you will gradually develop your gardener's eye. This is not something you can learn in a year, but you will start to see what looks good where and what colors work harmoniously together, and then begin to define how your garden should change from season to season. This is a process that continues to develop over a lifetime.

Much of this can be learned simply by observing nature. You will see what is proper for the seasons in your area by observing what grows naturally. What grows in the woods in spring? What grows in an unmown meadow in summer? What is blooming in the shade in September? What is the first plant to bloom each year? These observations will lead you toward a feeling for what you should be doing in your garden in accordance with the climate where you live. Plants have developed their growth habits over millions of years to conform to nature, and we should, for the most part, follow their examples.

I remember awakening on a train in Italy after an all-night ride from Paris. The last sight we had seen the night before was the wonderful yellow mustard fields around Dijon. The sight that greeted us that morning was mile after mile of the red poppies that grow wild all over Italy. These were not planted by any gardener, yet they were more glorious than the most ingeniously designed garden I have ever seen.

A rather disturbing development happened in the world of gardening in the eighteenth and nineteenth centuries. As global travel increased, people began to import tender plants from the subtropical regions, placing them in huge beds for masses of annual color. Many fine old and established perennial flower borders of native plants gave way to these interlopers, which, being totally unsuited for northern climates, were slain by the first frost. Consequently, removal and replacement were required.

Unfortunately, this practice is still going on, with the result that in spring and fall, the flower beds in city parks and even around many of our own homes more closely resemble newly dug graves than gardens. I believe it is a far better thing to depend largely on flowers that want to grow in our own areas than on those that we force to do so.

As you get used to working mainly with perennial plants, you will develop subtlety in your color schemes, in the way you use textures, and in your originality of arrangement. You will find yourself turning away from the rank magentas so often turned out by commercial plant breeders and toward the much purer pastels and primaries. You may come to enjoy the textures of winter in the garden . . . and plan for them. You will experiment. You will devise. You will improvise. You will invent. You will make mistakes.

You also will learn to edit, and to accept the fact that to do it, you will have to pull up or eradicate any plant that disturbs your sensibilities. This is not a sin. If a particular plant is troublesome or doesn't fit in with your evolving garden design, don't feel guilty about getting rid of it. Your intellectual satisfaction from creating your garden painting is more important than any common plant.

You will become a plantsman. (There is no such word as *plantswoman.* No matter what your gender, you are either a plantsman or you are not.) You will never be finished. This is because a garden is a living entity that changes constantly, not just day by day, but hour by hour, a living painting constantly evolving with the seasons. England's most famous and innovative garden designer, Gertrude Jekyll, wrote, in *A Gardener's Testament* (The Antique Collector's Club, 1982), "The duty we owe to our gardens . . . is to use plants that they shall form beautiful pictures."

"Something of the satisfaction of a good conscience," Jekyll said, "rewards and encourages the designer; for surely one of the objects of a good garden is that it shall be pictorially beautiful—that it shall be a series of enjoyable pictures painted with the living flowers."

I believe most gardeners with some vision learn to do this. Once you have transcended the narrow annual flower bed skirting the house and have created a perennial garden with some depth, you will inevitably compose pictures in it. Besides the joy of watching something you planted thrive and flower, there is also the satisfaction of watching your "painting" develop over the seasons and the years.

I find this to be a genuine religious experience. I hope you will find this same satisfaction and peace in a garden of your own.

Appendix A
The Catalogs vs. the Nursery

Let's assume, since you are a small-space gardener, that you're not going to be starting a lot of plants from seed. This takes a great deal of attention to detail, particularly for perennial plants, and can be quite time-consuming. Once, when I cultivated a much larger piece of land in Virginia, I asked a good friend to stay over at the house so that he could water my seedlings while I was out of town. "What trouble could it be to water a few plants?" he asked. He found out. I had 1,400 seedlings!

But these days I live in a big-city apartment and I get my plants from catalogs or nurseries. Which is better? I think the answer is twofold.

For bedding plants such as pansies, violas, impatiens, and the like, a nursery or garden center is certainly your best bet. Some catalogs will charge you for one plant what you would pay at a garden center for a dozen.

Do not look for common bedding plants such as marigolds, salvia, and impatiens in catalogs. They are usually not there. You will find only seeds. These plants are just too common to be profitable for most catalog houses. Again, shop at a nursery or garden center.

Most of the more common trees and shrubs also will be a better buy at a nursery. You will get larger plants that are used to being outdoors and won't need to be hardened off, the process of giving them progressively more sun each day until they're acclimated to the temperature.

That said, the positive side of catalogs for plants is choice. You will find an astounding variety of flowering plants available through the better catalogs that you will never, ever see in your local nursery. And if you are planning to have a garden with many specimen plantings for variety and interest, the catalog pages are where you should do a lot of your shopping.

Catalogs really excel over garden centers in bulbs, corms, and tubers. Tulips, daffodils, and virtually all other spring bulbs and corms need to be chilled for at least 8 to 12 weeks to perform properly. If they're not in the ground, they should be in the refrigerator. Now think back to the last time you saw all those spring bulbs at the garden center. Were they in the refrigerator? No, they were not! They were sitting on the shelves in brightly colored boxes at room temperature and exposed to light for weeks at a time. Room temperature is not going to help these bulbs perform at their best next spring. The catalog houses keep bulbs in big refrigerators until it's time for them to be planted, at which time they send them to you with the admonition to plant them right away. This is a better system.

The better catalogs are generally truthful, but be careful and use your head when looking them over. Sometimes a picture can be misleading. I recently saw a shot of some "red caladiums" in one of the more unreliable books. A couple of exotic-looking blooms were poking up through the red leaves. Of course, we know caladiums don't have flowers, don't we? Hmmm.

You will no doubt find many catalogs other than those listed here to fill your specialized needs. If you subscribe to magazines such as *American Horticulturist, Flower and Garden, Garden Design, Fine Gardening,* or *Horticulture,* you will see many ads for catalogs free for the asking. Ask.

PLANT CATALOGS

Here is a listing of some of my favorite catalogs:

W. Atlee Burpee & Co., 300 Park Avenue, Warminster, PA 18974; (800) 888-1447
This is a classic American seed catalog first published in 1876. Burpee has reliable merchandise at fair prices. Although primarily devoted to seeds, this book now offers many bulbs and seedlings. Burpee has bedding plants, too, although seedlings are readily available at any discount store.

Burpee does have competitive prices on perennial plants that can be difficult to start from seed, especially for apartment dwellers. (You may want to try starting a couple of things from seed just for something to occupy your gardener's mind during the winter. See the section in Chapter 17 on starting seeds indoors .)

Jackson & Perkins, 2518 South Pacific Highway, Medford, OR 97501; (800) 292-4769
Jackson & Perkins is probably the most famous purveyor of roses in the United States. Its catalog for spring features many selections of both new introductions and classics. If you are going to get hybrid tea roses by catalog, this is the place to shop. The winter catalog also contains lawn furniture, china, birdhouses, and bathroom gadgets.

J. W. Jung Seed Co., Randolph, WI 53957; (800) 247-5864
The greater part of this catalog is vegetables, but the company does have a nice selection of flowering plants and bulbs, and you can find some bargains, particularly on daylilies, which can be very expensive for the named varieties. There are also some good buys on lilies.

McClure & Zimmerman, 108 W. Winnebago, P.O. Box 368, Friesland, WI 53935; (414) 326-4220
This firm specializes in bulbs. Its merchandise is very high quality, and its prices are reasonable. This is a good source for unusual items such as species tulips. McClure & Zimmerman has the widest selection of these that I know of.

This is not a showpiece catalog. It is illustrated only with drawings, although these are very good quality.

Michigan Bulb Co., 1950 Waldorf, N.W., Grand Rapids, MI 49550; (616) 771-9500
This color catalog has a limited selection of plants and bulbs. The merchandise is fine, although sometimes of a smaller size than you would get elsewhere. In addition to flowers, trees, fruits, and vegetables, this company sells oddities such as the "Tomato Potato," a grafted Frankenstein that produces tomatoes above the soil and potatoes below. Egad!

Milaeger's Gardens, 4838 Douglas Avenue, Racine, WI 53402-2498; (800) 669-9956
Milaeger's produces a very good color catalog with good descriptive text and lots of cultural advice. It's a little different from all the others in that it lists many more varieties. The 1995 spring catalog listed an astounding 28 varieties of campanulas, 9 coreopsis, 8 digitalis, 31 chrysanthemums, and 14 veronica. In addition, Milaeger's has some unusual items not offered by other houses.

Orchids By Hausermann, 2N 134 Addison Road, Villa Park, IL 60181-1191; (708) 543-6855
This is a lovely full-color catalog with an incredibly diverse selection of the more well-known orchid varieties. The catalog I have features more than 125 varieties of *Phalaenopsis* alone! There is some choice in size, too, so if you are patient (meaning you can wait a year or so to see the blossoms), you can often get a choice variety rather inexpensively. Hausermann does not ship between December and March because of the cold weather, so if you want to give someone an orchid for the holidays, order early.

Park Seed Co., Cokesbury Road, Greenwood, SC 29647-0001; (800) 845-3369
Park Seed is an old and reliable firm with which I have done business for more than 20 years. I really like a firm that writes me a letter asking, "How was everything we sent you?" Park han-

dles high-quality seeds, bulbs, and plants, and stands behind its merchandise. If you don't like these people, you probably don't like anybody. Park has a very nice color catalog with helpful information. The spring catalog tends to concentrate on seeds rather than plants. The fall catalog offers many fine bulbs.

John Scheepers, Inc., P.O. Box 700, Bantam, CT 06750; (860) 567-0838

This firm specializes in bulbs and has a fine reputation. The catalog is well illustrated with color pictures. It contains a wide range of daffodils and some very unusual fritillaria. The prices are competitive, and there are some real bargains in lilies.

Van Bourgondien, 245 Farmingdale Road, P.O. Box 1000, Babylon, NY 11702; (800) 622-9997

This is a nicely illustrated color catalog, although the company does not offer as wide a choice as others listed here. Still, the merchandise is healthy when it arrives, and you can find some real bargains. This book is in wide distribution, so its descriptions are in pretty simple terms. You won't get much information on culture from the catalog, but Van Bourgondien is very good about sending cultural instructions with the merchandise.

Van Engelen Inc., Stillbrook Farm, 23 Tulip Drive, Bantam, CT 06750; (860) 567-8734

If you're in the market for a lot of bulbs, say 50 'King Alfred' daffodils or 100 'Big Ben' crocuses, this is the place to turn. Van Engelen sells in bulk and at bulk prices. If you have room for a large planting of tulips, daffodils, or whatever, shop here. This catalog is not illustrated, but the descriptions are good enough.

Venamy Orchids, Inc., Route 22, Brewster, NY 10509; (800) 362-3612

I don't believe Venamy has a real catalog, but it does have a listing of the many orchids it carries at more reasonable prices than most catalogs. I have three of these orchids, and I can vouch for the quality of the merchandise. With each plant you purchase, you will also get

extensive cultural information. But, please, take my advice: If you want to try an orchid, first try *Phalaenopsis*. It's easy to grow, you'll succeed with it, and you'll feel better about trying some others, all of which are more challenging.

Here's a tip. The phalaenopsis orchids you get from either Venamy or Smith & Hawken will be blooming size or actually in bud, and you can request the same from Hausermann. When you see an exceptionally cheap orchid in another catalog, check on the size. I recently saw a phalaenopsis advertised at a very good price. The fine print, however, revealed that it was small (a 2-in. pot). That's a very young plant and will not bloom for several years. If the catalog doesn't give the size, call the order department before you spend your money.

Wayside Gardens, Hodges, SC 29695-0001; (800) 845-1124

This is another top-of-the-line catalog offering superior stock. The catalog is beautifully illustrated but somewhat less inhibited than White Flower Farm's catalog. In the Wayside catalog, flowers are fairly gushing off the pages—ample-bosomed Georgia barmaids, shameless by comparison with their more demure cousins from Connecticut. There is plenty of information in this catalog: cultural and siting suggestions and lots of helpful descriptive notes. The spring catalog has quite a nice selection of English roses. The merchandise is healthy and arrives in good condition, although sometimes a bit on the late side for northern gardeners in the fall.

White Flower Farm, Route 63, Litchfield, CT 06759-0050; (800) 503-9624

This is the Mercedes-Benz of plant catalogs. It is lavishly illustrated on heavy stock and full of information and exceptionally good advice on siting, planting, and culture, delivered in a droll Connecticut Yankee tone of voice, purportedly by one "Amos Pettingill." The White Flower Farm catalog is the epitome of reservation. The pictures are not too bright, the varieties offered not too showy, the sample plantings perfectly understated. You will not always get a wide choice because the company insists on extensive testing before it offers any plant to the public. Nor will you get the showiest colors. The merchandise, however, is the best, and the cultural information is reliable. Accurate cultural information is important. Once I bought some lovely fall-blooming *Crocus goulimyi* from a catalog (not this company's), only to find out from a more reliable catalog that these plants like life best in Zone 9. My Zone 6 garden was the death of them.

TOOL AND ACCESSORY CATALOGS

Here is a listing of some of my favorite catalogs:

Gardeners Eden, P.O. Box 7307, San Francisco, CA 94120-7307; (800) 822-9600
This is a nicely illustrated catalog offering clothing for gardeners, garden tools and gadgets, decorative tiles, wicker furniture, some very expensive large fiberglass planters, and an occasional live plant. It is a fun book to look at and sometimes offers something you can't find anywhere else.

Gardener's Supply Company, 128 Intervale Road, Burlington, VT 05401; (800) 863-1700
This catalog has tools, pots, greenhouses, fountains, and anything else you might conceivably need for gardening. It has many things that are generally not available at your local garden center, including child-size tools.

Lee Valley Tools Ltd., P.O. Box 1780, Ogdensburg, NY 13669-0490; (800) 871-8158
If the White Flower Farm catalog is the Mercedes-Benz of plant catalogs, then Lee Valley is certainly the Jaguar of garden tool books. Its good, no-nonsense catalog is printed in four colors on heavy stock . . . great stuff at a fair price. Take particular notice of the absolutely beautiful transplant spade at half the price of another catalog. Check out the rain barrel system. Look at the variety of quality hoes. This book begs your consideration. Don't be put off by the fact that the catalog looks expensive; the merchandise isn't. It's a very nice read and a book you won't throw away.

Smith & Hawken, 25 Corte Madera, Mill Valley, CA 94941; (800) 776-3336
Smith & Hawken sells garden tools, furniture, and gadgetry—really *good* tools, furniture, and gadgetry. Its catalog also has lots of clothing, shoes, hats, and some live plants and bulbs. And you can find things in the Smith & Hawken catalog you can't find anywhere else, including some stunning flower pots. In some seasons, they offer very nice lily mixtures, sometimes preplanted bulbs, sometimes a selection of orchids, including the phalaenopsis. In some areas (not New York, where they seem to be in every florist's window), orchids are hard to find and Smith & Hawken would be a good source, as their merchandise is top-notch. But for a few regular pots or a trowel, just drive down to K-mart.

Smith & Hawken has a store in New York City's Soho district. When I asked why they would put a big garden store in the concrete canyons of Manhattan, they replied, "New York is our biggest market!" I guess that says something about the popularity of small-space gardening.

Appendix B
USDA Plant Hardiness Zone Map

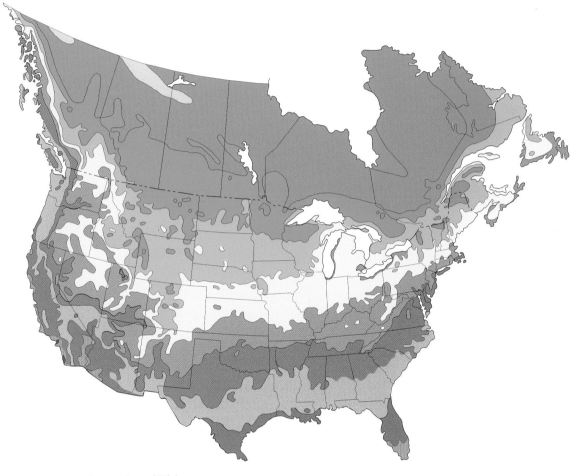

Average Annual Minimum Temperature by Zone

	Zone 1	below -50°F
	Zone 2	-40° to -50°F
	Zone 3	-30° to -40°F
	Zone 4	-20° to -30°F
	Zone 5	-10° to -20°F
	Zone 6	0° to -10°F
	Zone 7	10° to 0°F
	Zone 8	20° to 10°F
	Zone 9	30° to 20°F
	Zone 10	40° to 30°F
	Zone 11	50° to 40°F

This map shows the United States and Canada divided into 11 zones. To use the map, simply find the zone where you live and choose plants designated to grow well in your zone. Be aware, however, that other factors, including soil, exposure, moisture, and drainage, affect the growth of plants.

Index

PUBLISHER: Suzanne La Rosa
ASSOCIATE PUBLISHER: Helen Albert
EDITORIAL ASSISTANT: Cherilyn DeVries

EDITORS: Karen Weir-Jimerson, Barbara Jatkola
PROJECT MANAGER: Linda Glick Conway
DESIGNER: Jonathon Nix
ILLUSTRATOR: Elayne Sears
PHOTOGRAPHER (except where noted): Kerwin Fischer

TYPEFACES: Veljovic and Frutiger
PAPER: 70 lb. Patina
PRINTER: Quebecor Printing/Kingsport, Kingsport, Tennessee